WITHOUT GOD

WITHOUT GOD

MICHEL HOUELLEBECQ AND MATERIALIST HORROR

Louis Betty

The Pennsylvania State University Press | University Park, Pennsylvania

Library of Congress Cataloging-in-Publication Data

Names: Betty, Louis, author.
Title: Without God : Michel Houellebecq and materialist horror / Louis Betty.
Description: University Park, Pennsylvania : The Pennsylvania State University Press, [2016] | Includes bibliographical references and index.
Summary: "Addresses the religious, metaphysical, and existential dimensions of French novelist Michel Houellebecq's work. Argues that Houellebecq is the foremost contemporary chronicler of the spiritual anxieties of Western and specifically French modernity"—Provided by publisher.
Identifiers: LCCN 2016002369 | ISBN 9780271074085 (cloth : alk. paper)
Subjects: LCSH: Houellebecq, Michel—Criticism and interpretation. | Religion in literature. | Materialism in literature.
Classification: LCC PQ2668.077 Z57 2016 | DDC 843/.914—dc23
LC record available at http://lccn.loc.gov/2016002369

Printed in the United States of America
Published by
The Pennsylvania State University Press,
University Park, PA 16802–1003

The Pennsylvania State University Press is a member of the Association of American University Presses.

It is the policy of The Pennsylvania State University Press to use acid-free paper. Publications on uncoated stock satisfy the minimum requirements of American National Standard for Information Sciences—Permanence of Paper for Printed Library Material, ANSI Z39.48-1992.

This book is printed on paper that contains 30% post-consumer waste.

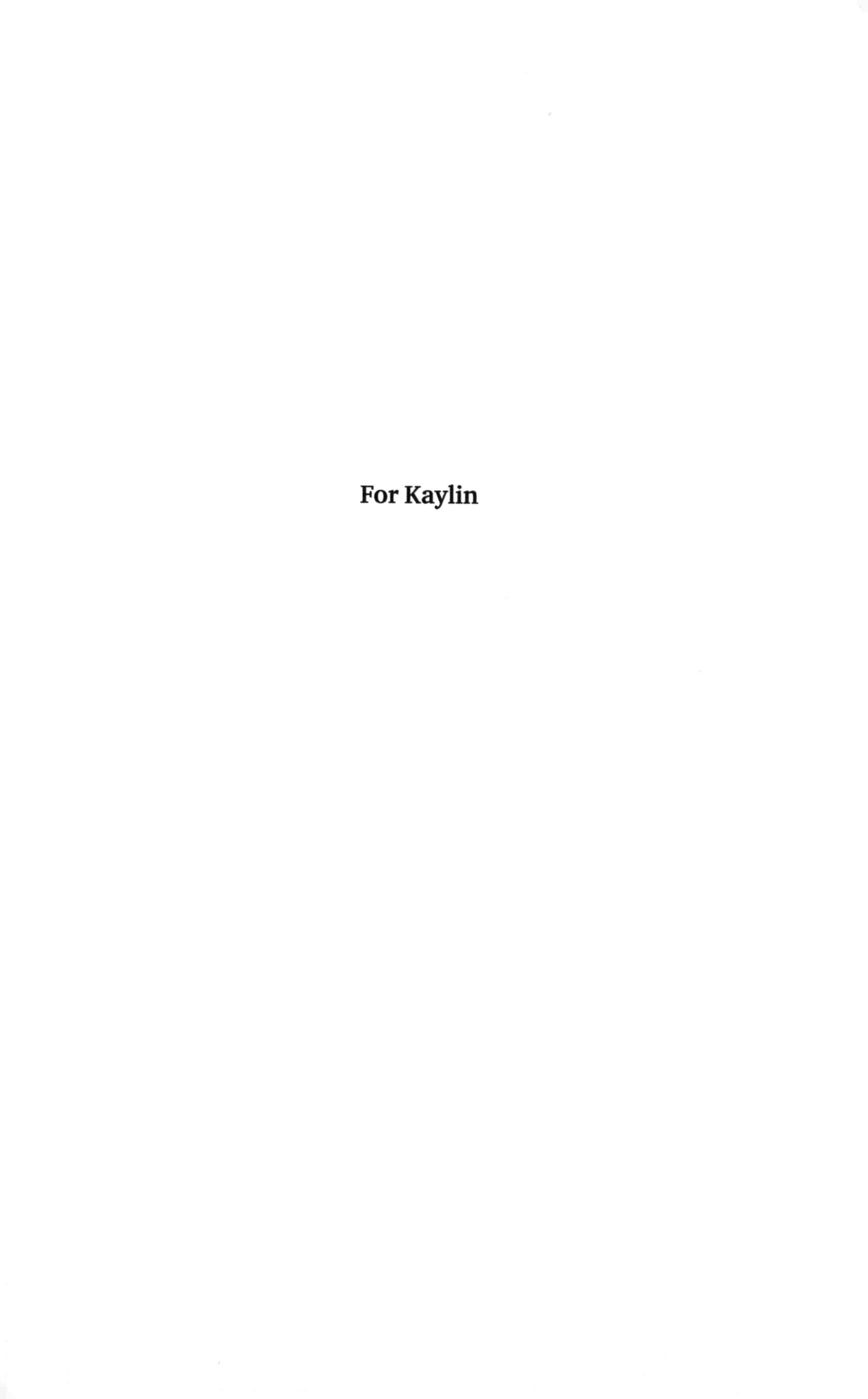

For Kaylin

Nothing more surely underlines an extreme weakness of mind than the failure to recognize the unhappiness of someone without God.

—**Pascal**

God doesn't exist, and even if you're stupid you end up realizing it.

—**Houellebecq (my translation)**

CONTENTS

Acknowledgments | ix

Introduction: The Houellebecquian Worldview | 1

1 Materialism and Secularism | 19

2 The Future of Religion | 47

3 Religion and Utopia | 75

4 Materialist Horror | 104

5 Liberalism Is God and the West Is Its Prophet | 122

Notes | 143

Works Cited | 149

Index | 156

ACKNOWLEDGMENTS

This book has been many years in the making, and I owe a tremendous debt of gratitude to the persons and institutions that have helped contribute to its final form. First I would like to thank Robert F. Barsky, a professor at Vanderbilt University, for his relentless support of my scholarship, as well as fellow members of the Vanderbilt French faculty, particularly Lynn Ramey and Virginia Scott. I also extend my gratitude to Michael Bess, Paul Lim, and Michel Pierssens, who provided valuable criticism during the earliest stages of this project, as well as to Vanderbilt University and the Department of French and Italian for their moral and material support of my work. Additionally, I want to convey my thanks to my employer, the University of Wisconsin at Whitewater, and specifically to Marilyn Durham and David Travis, who granted me valuable leave from teaching so that I could put the finishing touches on this book, and to my Whitewater colleagues who have supported my scholarly efforts, especially Jonathan Ivry. Finally, I want to thank the University of Wisconsin–Madison's Institute for Research in the Humanities, and specifically Susan Friedman, for giving me the opportunity to work as a research fellow at the institute during the 2014–2015 academic year; Kendra Boileau and Penn State Press for their careful stewardship of this project; and the reviewers who provided helpful and decisive feedback on an earlier version of this book.

Introduction

The Houellebecquian Worldview

Writing a book about Michel Houellebecq is a daunting task, if only because the scholarship dedicated to his work is in a constant state of evolution. When I began this project several years ago, there were no English-language monographs on Houellebecq; now there are at least four and probably more on the way. The present volume is intended as an addition to the scholarly contributions that came before it, some of which are of the highest quality. But it also aims to be more than that, as the pages that follow will bear out. It should come as little surprise that much of the work devoted to Houellebecq's fiction has centered on its sociopolitical meaning; the Anglo-American academy is still very much enamored of the political causes and controversies that shaped academic life beginning in the 1980s, and this is perhaps nowhere better reflected than in the contemporary study of literature. Carole Sweeney, for example, in her 2013 monograph, *Michel Houellebecq and the Literature of Despair*, has this to say about the essential significance of Houellebecq's work: "Houellebecq offers a withering critique of neoliberal late capitalism [. . .]. His fundamental concern is the encroachment of capitalism in its neoliberal biopolitical form into all areas of affective human life" (ix). By the term "biopolitical," Sweeney points to the sense in which market forces have supposedly tended to impose a kind of objectifying logic on domains of human existence, especially sexuality, that were formerly determined by more fluid, less rational criteria.

Houellebecq makes this point in his early fiction and nonfiction, perhaps most forcefully in *Whatever* (see 2009, 29–31, and 2011, 98–99), and it may in many respects be considered the cornerstone of the critique of neoliberal, late capitalist culture that we encounter in his texts. Indeed, as Bruno Viard has written in his book *Houellebecq au laser: La faute à Mai 68*, "Far from being a banality, the parallel traced [. . .] in *Whatever* between economic and sexual liberalism is totally unusual, and [. . .] constitutes the matrix of the Houellebecquian vision" (2008, 41, my translation). Other writers have echoed this sort of sociopolitical or politico-affective reading of Houellebecq's work, both in English- and French-language scholarship. In her article "L'Affaire Houellebecq: Ideological Crime and Fin de Millénaire Literary Scandal," Ruth Cruickshank contends, "The crime [of *The Elementary Particles*] is to challenge the dominant ideology depicted in the novel: the pursuit and production of desire in late capitalist society, an ideological foundation that can never bring satisfaction, but breeds isolation, competition and hatred" (2003, 113). On a similar note, Sabine van Wesemael has argued that Houellebecq is a reactionary novelist bent on using fiction to champion a return to traditional values: "The author takes pleasure in proclaiming a neoconservative reaction and pleads for adjustments to economic and sexual liberalism. Only a return to traditional norms and values (stay-at-home moms, restoration of the family and religion as the cornerstones of society) and a belief in the importance of science and technology for the improvement of the human species can save our expiring society" (2005, 89, my translation). From the very beginning, Houellebecq's fiction has raised interesting and often alarming political questions, with many scholars assigning themselves the difficult task of elucidating Houellebecq's often ambiguous and at times seemingly ambivalent engagement with both left and right.[1]

Of course, not all existing scholarship on Houellebecq is wholly given over to political and economic critique, and I certainly do not mean to suggest that such a way of reading Houellebecq is facile in comparison to other approaches. Douglas Morrey's 2013 analysis of Houellebecq's work as a contribution to contemporary debates about posthumanism, along with related French-language readings by such authors as Jean-François Chassay (2005), Laurence Dahan-Gaida (2003), and Kim Doré (2002), clearly demonstrates the diversity of responses that Houellebecq's fiction is able to evoke, especially at the intersection of science and literature. Similarly, a nearly exhaustive amount of work has been undertaken tracing the aesthetic and ideological debts Houellebecq owes to novelists and philosophers of the past. Zoë Roth (2012) has published a comparative study of Houellebecq and Bataille, while Gerald Moore (2011) has uncovered Houellebecq's problematic relationship with Nietzsche. Elements of intertextuality between Houellebecq and Baudelaire and between Houellebecq and Zola have received treatment from, respectively, Katherine Gantz (2005) and Sandrine Rabosseau (2007); another author has even suggested a similarity between Houellebecq's fiction and pro-religious discourse in Maximilien Robespierre's speech of 18 floréal an II (see Betty 2012).

In a more contemporary vein, Houellebecq's fiction has elicited comparisons with such present-day writers as Maurice Dantec, Richard Millet, Benoît Duteurtre, Philippe Muray, and Jonathan Littell. François Meyronnis (2007), for example, has written about the theme of extermination in these authors' works (most relevant for Houellebecq in *The Possibility of an Island* and, for obvious reasons, in Littell's *The Kindly Ones*), while François Ricard (1999) has characterized Houellebecq, Muray, and Duteurtre as writers bent on producing novels that are "against the world," that is, that take great care to skewer political correctness and the hypocrisy of both left and right, as well as to condemn our cultural obsessions with fun, insouciance, and endless festiveness. *Yale French Studies* has produced an issue subsuming work by Houellebecq, Dantec, and others under the heading *Turns to the Right?*, which wonders whether Houellebecq's apparent antifeminism or Dantec's gnostic apocalypticism do not constitute a reactionary element in contemporary French letters (see Johnson and Schehr 2009). The volume of writing on Houellebecq is so vast that I cannot possibly give a full account of it here; suffice it to point out that such sustained interested in a living European writer is rare in our time. Houellebecq's oeuvre is so broad in intellectual, ideological, and aesthetic content that he continues to appeal to a wide array of scholarly interests.

Nonetheless, my sense is that little complaint would be made in academic quarters if I were to suggest, in whatever context, that the concerns that have motivated the bulk of scholarship on Houellebecq tend to be social, political, economic, and essentially secular. Very little has been written about Houellebecq's complicated relationship with religion. Morrey (2013) has given the subject significant treatment, while Viard in *Les tiroirs de Michel Houellebecq* (2013b) has elucidated the importance of Comte and his *Religion of Humanity* in the exegesis of Houellebecq's texts. Cuenebroeck (2011), Chabert (2002), and Lloyd (2009) have addressed, respectively, the biblical structure of *The*

Possibility of an Island, Houellebecq's debts to positivism, and the redemptive power of love and Christian virtue in *Platform* and other Houellebecq texts; for my part, I have argued (2013) that Houellebecq's treatment of religious decline in his novels can be interpreted as a novelistic mise-en-scène of classical secularization theory. Aside from these few efforts, however, the religious, spiritual, and metaphysical dimensions of Houellebecq's fiction have gone largely ignored in the existing critical literature, with the religion question representing the principal blind spot in both English- and French-language academic treatments of Houellebecq's work. My purpose in this book is to correct this oversight, for I contend that Houellebecq is a deeply and unavoidably religious writer even if, as is clear from his numerous nonfiction remarks about God, he is probably agnostic himself. My interest in this volume is therefore to place Houellebecq's fiction in a much more metaphysical context than what has until now been attempted and to argue that the ills that plague his fictional universe stem less from (late) capitalism and the attendant social conditions to which it gives rise and more from the metaphysics of materialism that continues to enshrine and enable them.

Two works have called attention to the issue of materialism in Houellebecq's fiction, and though they do not go to the lengths I do in this book, they nonetheless accomplish the important task of setting a precedent for the reading I pursue. The first, Aurélien Bellanger's *Houellebecq, écrivain romantique*, includes a short chapter entitled "La dépression comme physicalisme" in which Bellanger makes a critical link between depression in Houellebecq's novels and the materialist, or physicalist, worldview that pervades them. With characters such as Djerzinski and *Whatever*'s narrator in mind, Bellanger writes, "The depressive experiences the world and himself as nonseparate: life for him no longer represents an exception in the universe, everything possesses the same nature [. . .]. Depression is nothing other than the awareness of scientific descriptions of the world. It is an emotional reaction to scientific knowledge" (2010, 162, my translation).[2] In a world where everything can be reduced to physical description, where free will yields to mechanism—where, as Bellanger adds, "[c]onsciousness is but a relatively recent cry in the dreadful tragedy of atoms" (162)—depression is the natural result of one's coming to terms with the facts of the physical universe. "Physics describes a world where everything is certain, where nothing is possible" (163). Life whittled down to the play of atoms thus represents a kind of materialist horror, and characters unable to see the world in anything but physicalist terms are inevitably prey to depression and suicide.

Ben Jeffery's *Anti-Matter: Michel Houellebecq and Depressive Realism* offers an equally judicious verdict on the existential havoc wrought by materialism in Houellebecq's fiction. Jeffery writes,

> The villainy of materialism is that it undermines [things that find their best expression in nonbiological, nonmaterial terms]: for instance, when it tells us that love is only a disguise for the urge to reproduce. Along this road we lose the use of a very fundamental and comforting terminology, or at least are obliged to admit that it gives a false or misleading account of human behavior. It emerges that there is basically no getting over yourself, no escaping your skull—and the more you are led to feel this way the more inclined you are to see life as isolated and vanishing. (2011, 34)

Materialism not only eradicates spirituality and transcendence, but also destroys the comforts of ordinary language. Terms such as "love," "friendship," and "affection" become meaningless; commonsense humanistic language is exposed as an unreliable system of description, which in due course will yield to a purely evolutionary or neurobiological account of human behavior. Moreover, the reduction of the human to the material, of the spirit to the body, vastly diminishes the meaning that one can assign to a given life. Jeffery adds, "Houellebecq's men don't think about God. All they think about—all there is—are the dictates of their biology, and their diminishing capacities to meet them. It is as if to say: the facts are what they are. So long as the facts are in your favor you can be happy, but there's nothing else to it" (34). As I demonstrate later on, this simple calculation—that the capacity for happiness rests solely in the body's ability to satisfy its instincts—lies at the heart of the existential despair that many, and likely most, of Houellebecq's characters endure.

One of the principal contentions of this book is that Houellebecq's novels represent a kind of fictional experiment in the death of God. And this experiment is best understood as a confrontation between two radically opposed domains: the materialism of modern science and the desire for transcendence and survival, which is best expressed in and through religion. The term "experiment" naturally evokes a comparison with the experimental style of Zola, but I want to distance myself from such an association. Zola's interest was to confront his characters with the inexorabilities of their biological and environmental conditioning. Houellebecq shares this interest to some degree, but only insofar as the implied determinism can be placed under a broader metaphysical canopy. Heredity and environment are not, to be exact, Houellebecq's central concerns; he is interested in God's absence and the submission to matter that such absence demands, which deprives human life of a meaning that might escape its immediate conditioning. In this sense, Houellebecq might be considered, if only to a limited extent, a more metaphysical Zola. The term "experiment" also accomplishes the useful task of curbing the quantity of realism one may feel compelled to read into Houellebecq's work. However realist in style they may be, novels such as *The Elementary Particles* and *The Possibility of an Island* should only very cautiously be taken to offer representative portrayals of contemporary European religiosity. As is now common knowledge, most Europeans remain "religious" in various ways, and since the 1980s sociologists of religion have been forced to admit that modernity and religion are not so mutually exclusive as was believed in the nineteenth century. These are points I expand on later; for now, it is sufficient to point out that approaching Houellebecq's novels as experiments will help to avoid the thorny issue of having to assess the truthfulness of their polemical content. Whether Houellebecq is "right" in his assessments of religion in Europe—or, for that matter, of contemporary sexuality or of the cultural consequences of May 1968—is not of chief concern. Rather, his novels serve as a means to explore the social and psychological consequences of a possible interpretation of historical, philosophical, scientific, and ideological developments in Western civilization and the cultural climate they have allegedly produced. In other words, Houellebecq's universe is intelligible from a certain point of view, even if it is not accurate.

I hope that my insistence in this book on the religion question compels scholars to think differently about Houellebecq as a writer and also about the stakes involved in the study of religion and literature. Throughout his career, Houellebecq has identified himself as either an atheist or an agnostic, and perhaps scholars have taken this as an indication that the treatment of religion in his novels is unworthy of serious investigation. Additionally, Houellebecq's fiction seems at least more overtly to be about other, somewhat more politically, sociologically, or anthropologically titillating subjects: sex tourism, cloning, the atomizing forces of capitalism, the shortcomings of feminism, to name only a few. Nothing, however, runs through Houellebecq's novels more clearly than his Comtean intuition that a society cut off from religion cannot survive, which Houellebecq affirms in a 2015 interview with the *Paris Review*. Herein lies the deep transgressiveness of

Houellebecq's work: the suggestion, utterly antithetical to the French doctrine of secularism (*laïcité*), that religion is a necessary element of social cohesion and happiness. And not just any sort of religion, either. Here again, Houellebecq sins against contemporary sensibilities. For instance, much writing on secularism in literature or the postmodern sacred has attempted to recuperate the notion of "sacredness" in a post-theological and postdoctrinal cultural landscape in which traditional constructs such as an all-powerful, all-loving God, the existence of an eternal soul, and the supernatural more generally have fallen out of favor. Amy Hungerford's (2010) notion of a "belief in meaninglessness," for instance, provides a case in point: rational, empirical constructs such as "deity" and "soul" may have been discredited, but one can still uncover novel forms of sacredness in language, metaphor, nature, and the human hunger for transcendence. Worthy as such efforts may be, Houellebecq will have nothing to do with them. Instead, he brings the religion question back to what he believes to be its heart: a concern not with sacredness but with *survival*. A religion that does not promise victory over death is doomed; we may sanctify all we want, but without a promise of material survival, we can hope to save neither the world nor ourselves.

Finally, I should say something about Houellebecq's place in the landscape of contemporary French letters, since it is in many respects unique. A consensus has emerged among many in the French literati that today's hexagonal literature is, to put the matter bluntly, not very good: it is mired in an obsession with hollow formalisms and stylistic trivialities; it is self-absorbed, solipsistic, and fails to engage society, religion, and politics; and, perhaps most damningly, its self-referentiality and more general failure to have anything to say makes it "too French," that is, totally "inexportable" (Bardolle 2004, 13). The reasons assigned to this literary atrophy are multiple. Tzvetan Todorov (2007), for instance, blames the legacy of structuralism and its excessive preoccupation with language.[3] Olivier Bardolle (2004) and Donald Morrison (2010) bemoan the triviality of the plots and characters that animate the average French novel, where often the most exciting action the reader can expect arises from a love triangle, a love quadrangle, or whatever geometrical configuration in which the protagonists may choose to erotically disport themselves. Pierre Jourde (2002) insists that French literature lacks guts, while Bruno Viard in *Littérature et déchirure* makes the shattering claim that "it is not certain that, since the Renaissance, French letters have known such discredit" (2013a, 11, my translation). Houellebecq has added to these refrains, writing in *Interventions II*,

> I have never been able to witness without a pang of anguish the technical extravagancy put to use by such and such a *formaliste-Minuit*[4] for such a paltry end result. In order to cope, I've often repeated this phrase of Schopenhauer: "The first and practically only condition for good style is having something to say." With its characteristic brutality, this phrase can be helpful. For example, during a literary discussion, when the word "writing" [écriture] is uttered, you know that it's time to relax a little bit, look around, order another beer. (2009, 153, my translation)

As I hope to show throughout, Houellebecq is an author who very clearly has something to say—about social life in contemporary France, about the economic future of Europe in the twenty-first century, about sexuality, and, most important for my purposes, about religion. This is not to suggest that Houellebecq is the only French author of his time to escape the solipsism and stylistic fetishes that Todorov and others deplore.[5] He is, nonetheless, the most *en vue*, both in France and abroad, among his like-minded contemporaries—hence this book.

Materialist Horror and the Question of Capitalism

In pursuing the reading I have outlined, I do not, of course, mean to imply that the critique of liberalism—and specifically of American liberal economics—that is found either implicitly or explicitly expressed in Houellebecq's fiction is less worthy of scholarly consideration. Indeed, central to the Houellebecquian worldview is the contention that the economic and sexual liberalism that emerged in France in the wake of the 1960s (and that, one might argue, marked the end of the Trente Glorieuses) has been a disaster for French culture and that the blame for this disaster rests squarely with the United States of America. At multiple places in his texts, Houellebecq unequivocally associates the process of Europe's "Americanization" with the liberal sexual practices exported to Western Europe by the American entertainment industry. For instance, in *The Elementary Particles*, Houellebecq writes,

> It was precisely at this time [the 1960s] that the consumption of prurient mass-market entertainment from North America [. . .] was spreading all over Western Europe. Along with the refrigerators

and washing machines designed to make for a happy couple came the transistor radio and the record player, which would teach the adolescent how to *flirt.* The distinction between true love and flirtation, latent during the sixties, exploded in the early seventies in magazines like *Mademoiselle Âge Tendre* and *Vingt Ans*, and crystallized around the central question of the era: "How far can you go before you get married?" The libidinal, hedonistic American option received great support from the liberal press. (2000a, 47)

The link suggested here between a liberal, consumer-driven economy and liberalized sexual practices informs perhaps the entirety of Houellebecq's complaint about sexuality in an Americanized Western Europe. The liberalization of sexuality is simply the next step in the evolution of capitalism: as soon as the market enshrined the individual as the basic economic unit of society, it was only a matter of time before the logic of competition was extended from the economic to the affective sphere, thus creating a new domain of struggle where a minimum of sexual satisfaction is no more guaranteed than a minimum of material comfort. In a much-cited example, the narrator of *Whatever*, having not made love for two years, laments the commodification of eroticism and the phenomenon of sexual pauperization that it has produced:

> In societies like ours sex truly represents a second system of differentiation, completely independent of money; and as a system of differentiation it functions just as mercilessly. The effects of these two systems are, furthermore, strictly equivalent. Just like unrestrained economic liberalism, and for similar reasons, sexual liberalism produces phenomena of *absolute pauperization.* Some men make love every day; others five or six times in their life, or never. Some make love with dozens of women; others with none. It's what's known as "the law of the market." (2011, 99)

Houellebecq's dour treatment of American liberalism closely accompanies his portrayal of contemporary sexual practices. Individualism and free choice, the ideological cornerstones of liberal economics, have produced a generation of Westerners who are so focused on their own individual needs and rights that they no longer know how to give pleasure to others. Unable to experience sexual gratification, men and women in Houellebecq's fiction turn to sadomasochism or the humiliations of group sex,[6] or, as in *Platform*, they abandon Europe to seek physical gratification among the prostitutes of Southeast Asia: "Offering your body as an object of pleasure, giving pleasure unselfishly: that's what Westerners don't know how to do anymore [. . .]. We have become cold, rational, acutely conscious of our individual existence and our rights. [. . .] we want to avoid alienation and dependence; on top of that, we're obsessed with health and hygiene. These are hardly ideal conditions in which to make love" (2002, 174–75). The liberal American model has not simply created an unjust economic system. Sexuality, too, has succumbed to radical individualism and an ensuing narcissism with the result that sexual satisfaction, which is dependent on intimacy, sharing, and a feeling of dependence, has become, to again evoke *Whatever*'s narrator, progressively impossible.

As compelling as this interpretation may seem, it would no doubt be simplistic to assume that the Houellebecquian critique of liberalism begins and ends with a treatment and subsequent repudiation of American liberal economics. At least superficially, Houellebecq's depiction of the miseries of "liberated" sexuality (that is, sexuality subject to the laws of the market) suggests a causal scenario in which the commodification of eroticism brought about by Europe's Americanization post-1968 has led to the "materialist horror" of a completely liberal sexual economy, where both currency and flesh are traded on the open market. In other words, a burgeoning materialism, especially in the domain of the erotic, would seem to follow on the heels of liberalism. Houellebecq often indicates as much, as this passage from *Interventions II* demonstrates:

> In terms of romantic relationships, the parameters of sexual exchange had also for a long time stemmed from a hardly reliable system of lyrical, impressionistic description. It was once again from the United States that the first serious attempt at defining standards was to come. Based on simple, objectively verifiable criteria (age, height, weight, waist-to-hip-to-chest ratio for women; age, height, weight, size of erect penis for men), it was first popularized by the porno industry and quickly adopted by women's magazines. If simplified economic hierarchy was for a long time the object of sporadic opposition [. . .] it's to be noted that erotic hierarchy, perceived as more natural, was rapidly internalized and became straightaway a matter of broad consensus. (30, my translation)

However, the causality I propose, which does justice to the totality of the Houellebecquian worldview, is one in which materialism—conceived of as a generalized belief in matter, which in its political manifestations contributes to the rise of ideologies as diverse as communism, fascism, and liberalism—represents the true menace to human relationships and sexuality in Houellebecq's novels. From this point of view, the gradual erosion of the theological conception of the human being, which began with the scientific revolution and reached its apex in the twentieth century, has given rise to a social order in which the value of human life is restricted to the parameters of economic exchange—that is, the human being is understood in essentially economic terms. One's attractiveness and even lovability are determined by indisputable criteria of market value, as if the human being were no different, in principle, from any other consumer product. This economic reduction of human value is fed by the materialism of modern science, which dismisses the possibility of free will and reduces the human being to a haphazard, fleeting collection of elementary particles. Humanism, which attempts to assign people rights in the absence of a deity capable of legitimating the moral order, does not stand a chance in these conditions. In the epilogue to *The Elementary Particles*, the novel's clone narrator laments the impotence of atheistic humanism: "It is important to remember how central the notions of 'personal freedom,' 'human dignity' and 'progress' were to people in the age of materialism [. . .]. The confused and arbitrary nature of these ideas meant, of course, that they had little practical or social function—which might explain why human history from the fifteenth to the twentieth century was characterized by progressive decline and disintegration" (258–59).

Aside from modern liberalism, all humanistic attempts to organize society according to nontheological principles (Marxism, socialism, communism, etc.) have been failures, and if the liberal model has succeeded, this is only because it is the most natural form of social organization, and thus the worst (see Houellebecq 2011, 124–25). The unbinding of humanity from God lies at the heart of the historical narrative the reader encounters in Houellebecq's work: lacking a set of moral principles legitimated by a higher power and unable to find meaningful answers to existential questions, human beings descend into selfishness and narcissism and can only stymie their mortal terror by recourse to the carnal distractions of sexuality. Modern capitalism is the mode of social organization best suited to, and best suited to maintain, such a worldview. Materialism—that is, the limiting of all that is real to the physical, which rules out the existence of God, soul, and spirit and with them any transcendent meaning to human life—thus produces an environment in which consumption becomes the norm. Such is the historical narrative that Houellebecq's fiction enacts, with modern economic liberalism emerging as the last, devastating consequence of humanity's despiritualization.

"Materialist horror" is the term most appropriate to describe this worldview, for what readers discover throughout Houellebecq's fiction are societies and persons in which the terminal social and psychological consequences of materialism are being played out.[7] It is little wonder, then, that these texts are so often apocalyptic in tone. *The Elementary Particles* and *The Possibility of an Island*, for example, depict the outright disappearance of a depressive and morally derelict human race. Desplechin, Djerzinski's colleague in *Particles*, says of the decline of Western civilization at the turn of the twenty-first century: "There is no power in the world—economic, political, religious or social—that can compete with rational certainty. The West has sacrificed everything to this need: religion, happiness, hope—and, finally, its own life. You have to remember that when passing judgment on Western civilization" (221). Similarly, in *The Map and the Territory*, Jed's final art project throws a veil of extinction not just on Western civilization but on humanity in general:

> The work that occupied the last years of Jed Martin's life can be seen [. . .] as a nostalgic meditation on the end of the industrial age in Europe, and, more generally, on the perishable and transitory nature of any human industry. This interpretation is, however, inadequate when one tries to make sense of the unease that grips us on seeing those pathetic Playmobil-type figurines, lost in the middle of an abstract and immense futurist city, a city which itself crumbles and falls apart then seems gradually to be scattered across the immense vegetation [. . .]. The feeling of desolation, too [. . .] as the portraits of the human beings who had accompanied Jed through his earthly life fall apart under the impact of bad weather, then decompose and disappear, seeming [. . .] to make themselves the symbols of the generalized extinction of the human species. They sink and seem for an instant to put up a struggle, before being suffocated by the superimposed layers of plants. There remains only the grass swaying in the wind. The triumph of vegetation is total. (2012, 269)

The Map and the Territory is in many respects the culmination of an evolution that begins with the posthuman, utopian ambitions of *The Elementary*

Particles and ends in this novel with a repudiation of utopian dreams in favor of a premodern and traditionalist solution to contemporary existential malaise. As I argue in chapter 3, the evolution across the span of Houellebecq's novels can be best understood as a progressive disenchantment with utopianism, accompanied by an ever-increasing sense of the oppressiveness of matter. The result of this evolution, as it is somewhat tentatively expressed in *The Map and the Territory* but then much more radically in *Submission*, is a wholesale abandonment of liberalism as a guiding principle for the organization of human social ife.

Before moving on, I should also say something about Houellebecq's reception in the United States, since this monograph is (to my knowledge) the first American attempt at a book-length study of Houellebecq's work. Houellebecq's novels have enjoyed broad success in the United Kingdom, a fact that no doubt explains the proliferation of studies on the author by British scholars. In the United States, however, much of the engagement with Houellebecq's work has come from reviewers who have generally been so repulsed by his fiction that they have had difficulty concealing their contempt. In his review of *The Possibility of an Island*, John Updike (2006, n.p.) writes that Houellebecq's "will to generalize smothers the real world under a blanket condemnation," and "the sensations that [he] gives us are not nutritive." Janet Maslin in the *New York Times* (2003) has described *Platform* as a "polarizing, audacious document rather than a viable novel," while Michiko Kakutani, also in the *New York Times*, says of *The Elementary Particles*, "As a piece of writing, [it] feels like a bad, self-conscious pastiche of Camus, Foucault and Bret Easton Ellis. And as a philosophical tract, it evinces a fiercely nihilistic, anti-humanistic vision built upon gross generalizations and ridiculously phony logic. It is a deeply repugnant read" (2000, n.p.). These reviews overlook much of the aesthetically and intellectually noteworthy qualities of Houellebecq's work and may bespeak, at least at some level, a typically American, perhaps even puritanical, response to a literary exercise steeped in irony, cynicism, and decadent excess. Even so, it remains true that few authors working today demonstrate the consistent ability to displease that Houellebecq has mastered, not to mention his eagerness to flout the benchmarks of political correctness.

Houellebecq's novels engage delicate social and political issues head on—Islam, sexual liberalism, technology, posthumanism, immigration, and violence in the banlieue, to name but a few—and in their treatment of those issues these texts often manifest a bullying lack of concern for the presumed political sensitivities of their audience. Indeed, it is difficult not to feel a certain ideological discomfort when Daniel says of Esther in *Possibility of an Island* that "[l]ike all very pretty young girls she was basically only good for fucking" (2007, 152), or when the openly racist character Robert in *Platform* praises the "elasticity" of certain components of Thai women's anatomy (2002, 80). Similarly, when, in *The Map and the Territory*, Houellebecq describes a West African housekeeper as "cantankerous and nasty" (2012, 8) and suggests that she "most probably stole from the shopping allowance" (8), the ideological censor in all of us cannot help registering some degree of alarm.

The atmosphere of sanctimony and recrimination that has surrounded the publication of Houellebecq's novels is remarkable, and even the critics most engaged with his work have been careful to issue the requisite condemnation of the author's seemingly egregious neglect of political decency. Murielle Lucie Clément, for example, writes in her article "Le héros houellebecquien," "The day has come to realize that what we may take to be hilarious witticisms is none other than an ideology deeply rooted in xenophobia, racism, and misogyny" (2006, 97, my translation). Little good is accomplished by trying to defend Houellebecq against such accusations. I only suggest that the sexism, racism, xenophobia, and perhaps homophobia that somewhat more than intermittently crop up in Houellebecq's novels ought to be subsumed under a general misanthropy; the real interest of his writing lies elsewhere.

Chapter Summaries

This book is divided into five chapters, each of which tackles a specific set of issues related to the religious, philosophical, and metaphysical dimensions of Houellebecq's work, as well as its relation to French intellectual and literary traditions. Houellebecq's fiction engages a wide variety of intellectual and academic domains, including quantum physics, sociology of religion, and utopian socialism, and it has been necessary throughout the course of this undertaking to address the myriad theories and ideas that find life in Houellebecq's texts. Readers of this book will encounter discussions of such subjects as the mind-body problem, positivism, quantum physics, and sociological theories of religion and secularization, as well as mentions of such diverse figures in the history of ideas as Charles Fourier, Maximilien

Robespierre, Émile Durkheim, Blaise Pascal, Clifford Geertz, and Talal Asad. Ultimately, this book not only serves to provide a careful exegesis of Houellebecq's texts, but also situates the author's engagement with religion,[8] theology, and philosophy within the broader context of the history of ideas, both French and Anglo-American. My approach is not intended to ignore the literary or performative dimensions of Houellebecq's novels, however much Houellebecq may tend at certain places to engage ideas polemically rather than performatively. Rather, as will be clear in subsequent chapters, the intellectual content of Houellebecq's fiction finds its fullest expression in his stories and characters, which make it worth reading. I offer the following chapter summaries in order to give the reader a clear indication of the direction my comments will take.

In chapter 1, I address Houellebecq's use of science in his novels and also argue that Houellebecq's texts present a novelistic mise-en-scène of classical secularization theory. On the one hand, I explore the ways in which materialism and science inform the aesthetic and ideological landscape of *The Elementary Particles*, in particular the novel's suggestions that quantum physics may have some application to human biological systems and that human nature might be improved by prevailing upon quantum physics in the fabrication of a new human genome. I contend that, while the science supporting the novel's vision of a posthuman future is questionable, it nonetheless offers a compelling metaphor for human relations no longer plagued by narcissism, excessive individualism, and physical separation. Second, I argue that Houellebecq's rendering of an irremediably secular West is in fact a fictional enactment of classical secularization theory, which erroneously holds that modernity and science are incompatible with religion and religious belief. Houellebecq's novels explore in experimental rather than in realistic or sociological fashion the social and psychological consequences of atheism; far from being so much "bad sociology," these novels are keen examinations of the lives of men and of societies that no longer lie beneath a sacred canopy.

In chapter 2, I explore Houellebecq's treatment of new religious movements and the prospects for religious innovation in officially secular states such as France. In *The Possibility of an Island*, Houellebecq imagines a future European society in which a cloning cult known as Elohimism (based on the Raelian sect that was founded in France in 1974 by the former race-car driver Claude Vorilhon)[9] has supplanted Christianity and Islam to become the Old World's leading religion. The sect promises its adherents immortality through cloning and machine-mind transfer and preaches a cult of youth that limits the meaning of existence to the gratification of sexual and other physical desires. I discuss the beliefs and practices of the Elohimite Church and investigate Elohimism's claims to religionhood based on classical Durkheimian understandings of religion, more recent formulations that locate the essence of religion in the supernatural, and definitions of religion that focus on its disciplinary and social-structuring, rather than its personal and individual, dimensions. In depicting the birth and rise of Elohimism in *The Possibility of an Island*, Houellebecq enters into a debate about the future of religious expression in an officially secular society and, more subtly, elaborates an alternative to an Islam that he (at least at the time of writing *Possibility*) finds abhorrent.

In chapter 3, I place Houellebecq's writing within the context of nineteenth-century pre-Marxist utopian thought. The utopian scenarios that Houellebecq entertains in novels such as *The Elementary Particles* and *The Possibility of an Island* borrow heavily from religious and quasi-religious nineteenth-century French utopianism, specifically the work of Auguste Comte. I examine the writing of utopians Charles Fourier, Claude-Henri de Saint-Simon, and Comte, as well as the revolutionary and religious discourse of Maximilien Robespierre, and read Houellebecq's portrayal of the posthuman utopias in certain of his novels in conjunction with these thinkers' work. Although the Houellebecquian utopia is in many respects an experimental choreography of Comtean positivism, Houellebecq faults Comte for failing to make provision for personal immortality in his religion of humanity and, accordingly, elaborates a quasi-religious response to a godless modernity in which immortality is achieved through cloning. However, by the end of *The Possibility of an Island*, Houellebecq abandons his utopian predilections, depicting the posthuman clone society in a state of even greater existential dereliction than is seen in twenty-first-century Western civilization. I also argue that Houellebecq's *The Map and the Territory* represents a break with the techno-religious utopianism that animates his previous works, with France finding salvation from economic ruin by abandoning industrialism and focusing its economy on tourism and a sort of "capitalism of the countryside," which caters to foreign tourists willing to pay handsomely to partake in the romanticized *art de vivre* that characterizes France's image abroad. I end by suggesting a link between France's "return to tradition" in the novel and a potential return to Catholicism, especially as it relates to the fictional Houellebecq's conversion to Catholicism just before he is murdered.

In chapter 4, I return to the concept of materialist horror and explore its philosophical foundations. I first offer a definition of the term based on my reading of Houellebecq in previous chapters and then point out some of its most memorable manifestations, focusing in particular on the novel *Whatever.* Crucially, I argue that the exaggerated nature of Houellebecq's depictions of contemporary social and moral decadence are to be understood as forms of experiment, wherein characters react in predictable ways to extremely unpropitious existential conditions—godlessness, extinction, and so on. Materialism provides the condition for the experiment, and horror is its result. Last, I draw several parallels between Houellebecq, H. P. Lovecraft, and Blaise Pascal and show how materialist horror as both a philosophical and aesthetic concept emerges from a comparative reading of Houellebecq and these two authors.

Finally, in chapter 5, I discuss Houellebecq's novel *Submission* and argue that it represents in many respects a culmination of Houellebecq's relentless critique of the shortcomings of liberal, Enlightenment civilization. From the collapse of Christianity to the misery of the modern "liberated" woman to the moral apathy and dissoluteness of the novel's protagonist, François, *Submission* explores the anxieties of modern freedom in the context of what may be their greatest threat: Islam. Far from being an "Islamophobic" text, *Submission* instead offers a kind of apologetics for a modern, Westernized Islam called upon to close the historical parenthesis opened by revolutionary civilization and to return humanity to a religiously grounded order. I argue that the novel's conclusion, in which François's conversion is described not in the narrative past tense but rather in the conditional, is an attempt on Houellebecq's part to implicate the reader in the text. In other words, *Submission* tempts those who have assumed Houellebecq's critique of liberal, secular civilization to follow that critique to its logical conclusion: conversion to Islam.

Houellebecq as Character: A Brief Consideration

One of the more consternating issues that has surrounded Houellebecq's novels is the seeming participation of the author in his own texts. From the very beginning, Houellebecq has embedded himself in his stories; the male protagonists of *The Elementary Particles* and *Platform* are both named Michel, while Houellebecq himself appears as a fictional character in *The Map and the Territory*. In some respects, this version of Houellebecq's novelistic apparitions seems an attempt by the author to outdo his critics in the media. For example, in the passages where Jed Martin meets Houellebecq in Ireland, the latter is depicted in terms so abject that any journalist offering a similar description might well be accused of defamation (see Houellebecq 2012, 100–101). Beyond the issue of any tête-à-tête with the media, however, such autobiographical flourishes give rise to a troubling question for critics and scholars: Is Houellebecq the man simply injecting himself into his novels in a more or less straightforward fashion—writing from what he knows, as it were—or is something rather the opposite taking place? Is it possible that Houellebecq's entire media persona is a kind of post hoc mirroring of the depressiveness, morbidity, and misanthropy of his characters? In other words, could it be that Houellebecq is having us on, that his novelistic polemics and his public comments—often phrased nearly word for word—are simply two sides of the same fictional enterprise?

I admit to having no evidence to suggest either conclusion, but I do want to issue a caveat concerning the latter viewpoint. Certainly a kind of "Houellebecq brand" has arisen in the popular imagination, that of the gloomy, chain-smoking provocateur lamenting his erotic failures and the agony of old age (see Riding 1999), and it is not out of the realm of possibility (far from it, I would imagine) that Houellebecq has exploited this image to sell his books. At the same time, critics should be careful not to credit Houellebecq with having the ambition, wherewithal, and foresight to accomplish such an unlikely, decades-spanning media coup. Not only does such a feat of media manipulation seem unlikely (France is not North Korea, and Houellebecq is not Kim Jong Un), but, proceeding from the more basic principle that one ought to avoid multiplying entities beyond what is necessary, it seems much more likely that Houellebecq is a serious writer with serious reasons for writing what he does. To conclude otherwise borders on conspiracy theorizing. I will state the matter simply: Michel Houellebecq has something to say in his novels. This does not mean, of course, that Houellebecq's texts are reducible to polemical tracts parading as fiction, but neither is their philosophical, ideological, and otherwise argumentative content strictly or necessarily ambiguous or "undecidable." Literature is allowed to be about something, and if Houellebecq chooses to embed himself in his novels, either overtly or covertly, he likely does so because it facilitates his task as a storyteller and a meaning maker. The opposite supposition would seem to assume the burden of proof.

Materialism and Secularism

Without a doubt, the twentieth century will remain in the eyes of the general public the age of triumph of the scientific explanation of the world, associated by it with a materialist worldview and the principle of local determinism.

—**Houellebecq 2009 (my translation)**

My goal in this chapter is twofold. First, I elucidate Houellebecq's use of science in his novels, and I demonstrate how the philosophical positions vis-à-vis materialism that he sketches out in his nonfiction are enacted in his fiction, most specifically in *The Elementary Particles*. Houellebecq has tended to entertain scientific and philosophical notions with a great deal of confidence, if not with rigor, enough to warrant a serious study of how they find expression in his novels. Second, because the assumption of a rampant materialism and attendant atheism constitutes a central tenet of the Houellebecquian treatment of modernity, in the remainder of this chapter my concern is with situating this particular treatment within the modern discourse of secularization that emerged during and after the Enlightenment.

Scholarship in the sociology of religion has cast significant doubt on the claim that modernity and religion are incompatible; indeed, some scholars have even declared the thesis defunct. Houellebecq, however, rather curiously employs the thesis as if it were self-evident, potentially leading to the criticism that his novels—or at least their representation of religion in contemporary Europe—are only so much bad sociology. I address this concern and argue that Houellebecq's mise-en-scène of classical secularization theory is in fact an experimental tactic deployed to explore the social and psychological consequences of outright atheism and the materialistic liberalism it enables.

Houellebecquian Materialism: A Qualified Case?

Michel Houellebecq's unflagging preoccupation with death, physical decline, suicide, determinism, and atheism is unique in contemporary literature. Indeed, it will come as little surprise to those most familiar with his work that at virtually no point in the Houellebecquian corpus does the reader encounter any or unqualified reference to transcendence or "spirit." In fact, the notion of spirit is specifically derided in certain passages. In *The Possibility of an Island*, Daniel, who is considering joining the New Age Elohimite Church, reflects,

> I had not only never held any religious belief, but I hadn't even envisaged the possibility of doing so. For me, things were exactly as they appeared to be: man was a species of animal, descended from other animal species through a tortuous and difficult process of evolution; he was made up of matter and configured in organs, and after his death these organs would decompose and transform into simpler molecules; no trace of brain activity would remain, nor of thought, nor of anything that might be described as a *spirit* or a *soul.* My atheism was so monolithic, so radical, that I had never been able to take these subjects completely seriously. During my days at secondary school, when I would debate with a Christian, a Muslim, or a Jew, I always had the impression that their beliefs were to be *taken ironically*; that they obviously didn't believe, in the proper sense of the term, in the reality of the dogmas they professed [. . .]. (2007, 178)

Such a point of view is not limited to Daniel. This same insensitivity to life's spiritual dimension is also apparent in characters such as Djerzinski and *Whatever*'s narrator. Of the former, Houellebecq writes, "Far removed from Christian notions of grace and redemption, unfamiliar with the concepts of freedom and compassion, Michel's worldview had grown pitiless and mechanical. Once the parameters of the interaction were defined, he thought [. . .] events took place in an empty, spiritless space [. . .]. What happened was meant to happen; it could not be otherwise; no one was to blame" (2000a, 75). And the nameless protagonist in Houellebecq's first novel says, "On Sunday morning I went out for a while in the neighborhood; I bought some raisin bread. The day was warm but a little sad, as Sundays often are in Paris, especially when one doesn't believe in God" (2011, 126). Subsequent developments in this text, in particular the narrator's statement that "the goal of life is missed" on the novel's final page, offer little indication that Houellebecq's anonymous character has given much consideration to his divine nature, however much his friend the priest Jean-Pierre may have urged him to earlier (30).

As is typical of Houellebecq, these sorts of pronouncement on godlessness are not limited to his novels' characters, but also enjoy polemical exposition in certain passages. *The Elementary Particles*, for example, makes a harrowing diagnosis of contemporary existential malaise:

> Contemporary consciousness is no longer equipped to deal with our mortality. Never in any other time, or in any other civilization, have people thought so much or so constantly about aging. Each individual has a simple view of the future: a time will come when the sum of pleasures that life has left to offer is outweighed by the sum of pain (one can actually feel the meter ticking, and it ticks always in the same direction). This weighing up of pleasure and pain, which everyone is forced to make sooner or later, leads logically, at a certain age, to suicide. (204)

This perspective is common to many of Houellebecq's characters. Annabelle of *Particles* commits suicide when she is diagnosed with uterine cancer (231); Bruno's girlfriend, Annick, jumps off a Parisian rooftop when her ugliness, along with Bruno's rejection of her, becomes insufferable (128). In the post-religious, materialist universe of Houellebecq's fiction, the earthbound sufferer is not to expect any heavenly recompense for his or her pains, and thus no relief from them at the thought of a better world to come. There is only matter, after which, annihilation.

The materialist worldview is central to the ways in which Houellebecq's characters live, suffer, and die, just as it is central to the decline and end of Western civilization that *The Elementary Particles* tracks. In much the same way that realism and naturalism inform Flaubert's and Zola's work, respectively, materialism represents the principal experimental condition of Houellebecq's fiction.[1] Much, if not all, of the pathos of the author's major characters—Bruno's sexual obsession and loathing for his mother, Djerzinski's antihumanist and antihuman creed, Daniel's fear of aging and impotence, the sexual alienation of the narrator in *Whatever* and of Michel in *Platform*, and even the resigned morbidity of the character Houellebecq in *The Map and the Territory*—is informed by a terror of separation, physical decline, and death in turn fueled by an obsessive awareness that "this is all there is." It is worth noting that Houellebecq participates in his characters' malaise. As he writes to Lévy in *Public Enemies*: "it's true that a world without God, with nothing, is enough [to] make anyone *freak out completely*" (2011, 139). The first reading of Houellebecq's work must therefore be a materialist reading, for outside of this basic assumption about the nature of reality, it becomes difficult to identify a sense of thematic and intellectual unity in his work.

As a philosophical concept, materialism denotes two methodologically distinct but formally and ideologically related domains. The first, attached to the continental tradition and most specifically to Marx (though also to Hegel and to Nietzsche's "genealogical" approach to history), evokes class struggle and the notion that human consciousness is determined by material and historical conditions beyond our immediate control. The second, which hails from the analytic tradition that emerged in the twentieth century in the work of philosophers such as Bertrand Russell and Ludwig Wittgenstein, but which may be traced all the way back to Descartes, relates strictly to the nature of the mind itself and forgoes the historical and economic considerations of Marxian theory. It is this second theory, which may be referred to as mind-body materialism or physicalism (a term first introduced in the 1930s by the Vienna Circle philosophers Otto Neurath and Rudolf Carnap), that is of interest in regard to Houellebecq. In the physicalist view, "immaterial" entities, such as spirit, soul, and gods, are premodern, prerational fantasies, and we have Descartes and his disastrous substance dualism to thank for them.[2] For the mind-body materialist, Descartes's immaterial mind is nothing more than the product of the brain: as the brain dies, so does the mind. As a consequence, mind-body materialism explains away traditionally immaterial entities as no more than complex arrangements of "elementary particles," and in doing so rules out all talk of such optimistic phenomena as spirit, soul, and the survival of physical death.

Houellebecq has denied in *Public Enemies* and elsewhere that he is a materialist in the sense described above, even while his novels are in large part explorations of the social and psychological consequences of the physicalist worldview. For example, in a 1998 interview with *Lire*, he says, "There's good news in [*The Elementary Particles*], no? The first is that materialism has had its day. It's disappearing, pulverized by something else that's yet to be defined" (Houellebecq 1998, n.p., my translation). Elsewhere in his nonfiction, Houellebecq has claimed that the very concept of matter is a metaphysical fantasy that came to replace God with the arrival of modern science (Houellebecq and Lévy 2011, 144), adding that discoveries that emerged in the twentieth century from quantum physics (phenomena such as action at a distance, nonseparability, and complementarity) require abandoning the notion of matter entirely. He writes in *Interventions II*, "The twentieth century will also remain that paradoxical era during which physicists refuted materialism, renounced local determinism, and as a matter of fact totally abandoned this ontology of objects and properties, which at the same time was spreading among the public as the basis of a scientific vision of the world" (2009, 155, my translation). As is often the case with Houellebecq, these public claims take on a performative aspect in his fiction, with *The Elementary Particles* serving as something of a mise-en-scène of these views. More important still, Houellebecq's second novel suggests that the remedy to the West's existential malaise may lie in an "ontological reconfiguration" brought on by the surpassing of materialism, accompanied and indeed facilitated by the application of quantum physics to the domain of molecular biology. Near the end of *The Elementary Particles*, Houellebecq writes apropos of the new civilization of clones and their rupture with their materialist past:

> *So, we now can listen to this story of a materialist era*
> *As an ancient human story.*
> *It is a sad story, but we will not be saddened by it*
> *Because we are no longer like these men.*
> *Born of their flesh and their desires, we have cast aside their categories and their affiliations,*
> *We do not feel their joys, neither do we feel their sufferings,*
> *We have set aside*

Indifferently
And without the least effort
Their universe of death. (247)

This finale, however, gives rise to a potentially serious confusion in the mind of the reader: How exactly is materialism surpassed, if the basis for doing so lies in the merely physical alteration of the human genome? In other words, does *The Elementary Particles* really deliver the goods—escape from spiritual and existential despair—that it promises to serve up? My contention is that it does not, and, if anything, the novel's finale even reinforces the materialism it seeks to subvert. This is not to say that the novel fails to offer a vision of a better world, or that the supposed science of "perfect reproduction" that the reader finds at its conclusion does not possess deep metaphorical significance. But an escape from materialism, *Particles* is not.

Quantum Uncertainties

Houellebecq's stance on materialism might seem of secondary interest to the literary scholar but for one thing: it deeply informs the scientific and philosophical discourse encountered in *The Elementary Particles*, if not throughout Houellebecq's writing. In his "Lettre à Lakis Proguidis," published in *L'Atelier du Roman* in 1997 as a response to an article on poetry and the novel by Proguidis, the founder of the review, Houellebecq describes the prevailing worldview of his time as "a materialist ontology" grounded in a concept of "local determinism" (2009, 152, my translation). In this perspective, material reality is describable in terms of rigidly mechanistic laws, which, if ascertained and applied with rigor, can be used to generate an exhaustive portrait of the universe. This is essentially the Newtonian view of reality inherited from the scientific revolution, with its attendant thermodynamic laws, natural constants, and Laplacian demon overseeing the entire operation. Elsewhere, however, in both his fiction and nonfiction, Houellebecq has contrasted the classical Newtonian view with a kind of quantum materialism—the notion that the laws of quantum physics and in particular the Copenhagen interpretation,[3] which suggests that physical reality has only a probabilistic, virtual existence, point in the direction of an altogether new ontology, which replaces the unbending, atomistic determinism of the Newtonian model.

And it is precisely this transition from a Newtonian to a quantum ontology that *The Elementary Particles* explores, with the latter being represented as a genuine remedy to the coldly deterministic, mechanical, and materialist worldview that supposedly prevails in our era. As I demonstrate below, the science supporting these developments is somewhat problematic; indeed, the novel even appears to grant its implausibility. For example, the novel's narrator claims near the book's end that Djerzinski's discoveries in genetics, which led to the creation of a new race of humans freed from the biological limitations of their forebears, rely at base on certain "risky interpretations" (251) of the principles of quantum physics. Nonetheless, Houellebecq's use of quantum physics in the novel furnishes him with the means of evoking the social and psychic pitfalls of contemporary materialism, as well as humanity's collective hopes for deliverance under the auspices of an altogether new understanding of reality.

From a philosophical point of view, quantum theory is interesting because it appears to radically reorient the relationship of the mind with the external world. The mind organizes experience in accordance with fundamental intuitions of space, time, and linear causality. But quantum wave functions—the "stuff" of quantum physics—exist in a dimension beyond what experience can capture. In his book *Taking the Quantum Leap*, philosopher Fred Alan Wolf describes the quantum universe:

> This [quantum] reality is a bridge between the world of the mind and the world of matter. Having attributes of both, it is a paradoxical and magical reality. In it, causality is strictly behaved. In other words, the laws of cause and effect manifest. The only problem is that it isn't objects that are following those laws (at least, not the ordinary kinds of objects we usually refer to), but ghosts! And these ghosts are downright paradoxical, able to appear in two or more places, even an infinite number of places, at the same time. When these ghosts are used to describe matter, they closely resemble waves. And that is why they were first called "matter waves." In modern usage, they are called "quantum wave functions." (1989, 184–86)

The basic posits of quantum theory are twofold. First, we cannot observe an electron wave/particle without interfering with it (and thus changing its state): the better we can see the electron (particle) in the microscope, the less we are able to say where it (the propagating wave) is going; yet, the better we can see where it is going, the less able we are to say where it is. This observational limitation is known as Heisenberg's uncertainty principle, and it has to do with the fact that the tool we use to look at electrons—light, which mediates our observation of objects—does things to the wave function that alter its state. Just what exactly is our observation doing? This brings me to point number two. According to the Copenhagen interpretation, our observation is literally bringing the "physical" electron into existence. Quantum wave functions are virtual entities, which, explained in terms we can make sense of, exist as a series of probabilities of an electron's location. When we shine a light on the wave function, it collapses and the electron appears at a specific location. When we are not looking, the wave reemerges and begins to propagate through space as a virtual entity.

It is important to keep in mind that terms like "virtual" are more metaphorical than anything else. Human observation does not actually call the world into being; what is happening is rather that the world is appearing to us in a way determined by internal intuitions that do not represent the external world as it really is—that is, as it is "quantumly." To experience the world as we do is to experience electrons as waves collapsing into particles. But what such objects (or waves or functions) do on their own time is their business, and our access to those activities is purely mathematical.

In some respects, the quantum theorists confirm scientifically what philosophers such as Kant already knew: the external world is not just "given" to the senses, but the mind has a way of representing it that may not do justice to actual, quantum states of affairs. As Kant writes in *Critique of Pure Reason*, "What may be the nature of objects considered as things in themselves and without reference to the receptivity of our sensibility is quite unknown to us. We know nothing more than our own mode of perceiving them, which is peculiar to us, and which [. . .] is so to the whole human race" (1990, 135). More important, quantum physics tells us that the seeming weirdness of quantum phenomena only manifests at the level of elementary particles. Theoretically, the wave functions of the electrons in the moon could suddenly cause the satellite to reorganize itself as a hulking mass of kitchen appliances. Such an occurrence is, in other words, a quantum possibility. But of course such things never happen, and never could happen, for it would take an eternity for the wave functions of such a large object to propagate to the point where even the most microscopic changes in the physical structure of the moon, or of any other object, could take place. Classical mechanics, though technically mistaken in light of quantum theory, therefore allows us to predict macrophysical events as if they were ruled by rigidly deterministic laws.

The Elementary Particles is eager to infer a causal link between the quantum uncertainty associated with the behavior of electrons, and the chemical and electrical events in macrophysical systems, such as the human brain. While Djerzinski may claim, for instance, that "the sheer number of neurons [. . .] statistically cancels out elementary differences, ensuring that human behavior is as rigorously determined [. . .] as any other natural system" (77), in the next moment he suggests that quantum events in the brain—specifically, "a different harmonic wave form [that] causes changes in the brain"—may give rise to acts of free will (77). In other places the novel focuses on the quantum wave function itself, more specifically on the notion that material reality may in fact be described as an infinity of ever-propagating, interpenetrating waves, which taken together weave all the particles of the universe into an inseparable whole. Houellebecq writes, "In an ontology of states the particles are indiscernible, and only a limited number are observable. The only entities which can be identified and named are wave functions and, through them, state vectors—from which arose the analogous possibility of giving new meaning to fraternity, sympathy and love" (248–49). This suggestion that the quantum behavior of elementary particles could have anything to do with fraternity, sympathy, and love is understandably confusing. Physical reality may be describable in terms of wave functions, but the careful reader will no doubt wonder how this description is expected to heal the wounds of physical separation that afflict the characters of *Particles*. Human beings are not electrons, and one wonders what possible relevance to human relationships and social organization quantum wave theory could possibly hold, beyond the purely metaphorical, especially when the link between the two domains is so evidently tenuous.

But here is precisely the moment to distinguish between Houellebecq's use of the quantum wave as an aesthetic metaphor for the social organization of his posthuman utopia, and the implementation of quantum principles in the creation of the novel's race of clones. In the second instance, the narrator explains, "Hubczejak rightly notes that Djerzinski's great leap lay not in his rejection of the idea of personal freedom [. . .] but in the fact that he was able, through somewhat risky interpretations of the postulates of quantum mechanics, to restore the conditions which make love possible" (251). Naturally, Houellebecq never discusses the science that would render these comments more intelligible—for presumably such science does not exist. How quantum mechanics, which describes the behavior of subatomic particles, could literally be brought to bear in the fabrication of a new human species is left splendidly unclear, and for this reason the novel's conclusion may strike some readers as disingenuous. In her monograph *Michel Houellebecq, le plaisir du texte,* Sabine van Wesemael writes, "[W]e can above all reproach Houellebecq for not furnishing the elements of a solution [in *The Elementary Particles*]. Clownish and absurd utopias, inspired by futuristic Nietzschean theories of the Superman (the clone) and by science fiction, offer no real resolution" (2005, 186, my translation). To make sense of the finale, it is instead necessary to regard Houellebecq's treatment of quantum physics less as scientific prognostication and more as a metaphor for improved human relations that, when understood correctly, takes *Particles* out of the domain of the clownish and offers a conclusion that is at once moving and serious. Houellebecq's concern in *Particles* is to make a point not about the exciting implications of quantum physics for biology, but rather about the horrors of social atomization, as this passage at the end of the novel bears out: "Having broken the filial chain that linked us to humanity, we [the clones] live on. Men consider us to be happy; it is certainly true that we have succeeded in overcoming the forces of egotism, cruelty and anger which they could not [. . .]. To humans of the old species, our world seems a paradise. We have even been known to refer to ourselves—with a certain humor—by the name they so long dreamed of: gods" (263).

The metaphorical scheme that Houellebecq has in mind finds expression in *Particles* in numerous places, perhaps the most important being Djerzinski's reaction to the rite performed during Bruno and Anne's wedding. Struck by the priest's depiction of "two bodies becoming one" in holy matrimony, Djerzinski quips,

> "I was very interested by what you were saying earlier . . ." The man of God smiled urbanely, then Michel began to talk about the Aspect experiments and the EPR paradox: how two particles, once united, are forever an inseparable whole, "which seems pretty much in keeping with what you were saying about one flesh." The priest's smile froze slightly. "What I'm trying to say," Michel went on enthusiastically, "is that from an ontological point of view, the pair can be assigned a single vector state in a Hilbert space." (144)

Here the novel suggests a metaphorical connection between the linking of human lives, as in marriage, and the discovery that electrons with the same vector in a "Hilbert space" will act instantaneously on each other even over immense distances (the principle of nonseparability).[4] Houellebecq no doubt intends the exchange between scientist and priest to be humorous, but we should not ignore the metaphorical depth, indeed the religious significance, of Djerzinski's remarks. Later, after Djerzinski is reunited with Annabelle, he has a dream: "he saw the mental aggregate of space and its opposite. He saw the mental conflict through which space was structured, and saw it disappear. He saw space as a thin line separating two spheres. In the first sphere there was being and separation, and in the second was nonbeing and the destruction of the individual. Calmly, without a moment's hesitation, he turned and walked toward the second sphere" (194). The first sphere is the world of determined physical interactions, the domain of mechanical cause and effect, where human minds and bodies are separated by immutable barriers of space, time, and embodiment. The second sphere is the quantum dimension: there, where all is woven together in an infinitely interpenetrating universe of quantum wave functions, the illusion of physical separation has been lifted.

It is precisely this vision that motivates Djerzinski's work in genetics. By sharing the same genetic code, his clones have achieved at least in some figurative sense the nonseparability of united electrons. Furthermore, in doing away with sexual reproduction, the sexual alienation that plagued the humans of the "age of materialism" has yielded to free love, pleasure liberated from jealousy and fear of rejection, and infinite belonging to and in the bodies of others. In his fictive monograph, *Meditations on Interweaving*, Djerzinski writes, "Love binds, and it binds forever. Good binds, while evil unravels. Separation is another word for evil; it is also another word for deceit. All that exists is a magnificent interweaving, vast and reciprocal" (251). If readers and critics alike can accept this vision for what it is—an idealistic, often satirical, yet heartfelt fantasy about the future of human relations—rather than dismiss it for its fuzzy use of science, Houellebecq's quantum future, far from coming off as clownish or absurd, should furnish a significant and thought-provoking counterpoint to the imperfect and imperfectible social relations of our time and, indeed, our species.

But does *The Elementary Particles* truly augur the transition from a materialist to a postmaterialist age? In both *Particles* and his nonfiction writing, Houellebecq has identified materialism writ large with the description of reality issuing from classical Newtonian mechanics—what one might think of as the materialism of a high school chemistry textbook, with electron orbs rotating around a red and blue clump of protons and neutrons. In "Lettre à Lakis Proguidis," Houellebecq argues that quantum physics constitutes a refutation of this kind of materialism: "The twentieth century will also remain that paradoxical era where physicists refuted materialism, swore off local determinism, totally abandoned [. . .] this ontology of objects and of properties, which at the same time was spreading among the general public as the basis for the scientific vision of the world" (2009, 152, my translation). *Particles* offers a nearly identical commentary: "materialism had had a historical importance: to break down the first barrier, which was God. Man, having done this, found himself plunged into doubt and distress. But now a second barrier had been broken down—this time in Copenhagen. Man no longer needed God, nor even the idea of an underlying reality" (249). In both of these passages, the propensity seems to be to conflate matter (what we generally think of as solids, liquids, and gases) with the broader notion of the material, which includes all that exists in the observable universe. The quantum wave function may not be material in the macroscopic sense—that is, in the way that a table is material—but to say that it is not material in the broad sense is mistaken. If anything of interest to the nonspecialist can be taken away from quantum mechanics, it is that the ultimate nature of the physical universe is stunningly mysterious. Much of the stuff of the universe is in fact energy: energy is not material in the commonsense understanding of the word, but no one would claim that its nature is not physical. *The Elementary Particles* therefore ends up reaffirming the materialism that it attempts to subvert. While one may, and in fact should, understand its finale metaphorically as an optimistic vision of a world no longer plagued by social atomization, it is important to avoid the understandable temptation to read it as a scientific program shrouded in a fictional guise.

Lifting the Sacred Canopy

Houellebecq's novels depict a West in which religion, and specifically Christianity, have succumbed to the rationalizing forces of modernity. Faith has yielded to science, dualism has yielded to materialism, and materialism has created a culture in which humanity is no longer able to find meaningful responses to existential questions about death, eternity, and ultimate value.

Religion is ever in danger of being vanquished by the vicissitudes of history. Daniel1 explains in *The Possibility of an Island*:

> In countries like Spain, Poland, and Ireland, social life and all behavior had been structured by a deeply rooted, unanimous, and immense Catholic faith for centuries, it determined morality as well as familial relations, conditioned all cultural and artistic productions, social hierarchies, conventions, and rules for living. In the space of a few years, in less than a generation, in an incredibly brief period of time, all this had disappeared, had evaporated into thin air. In these countries today no one believed in God anymore, or took account of him, or even remembered that they had once believed; and this had been achieved without difficulty, without conflict, without any kind of violence or protest, without even a real discussion, as easily as a heavy object, held back for some time by an external obstacle, returns as soon as you release it, to its position of equilibrium. (2007, 245)

Consumerism prospers in this post-religious civilization, since only it appears capable of furnishing the distractions that can divert human beings from the oppressive awareness of their mortality. Naturally, none of this can make up for the fundamental absence of spirituality haunting modernity, as Jean-Pierre Buvet, the priest in *Whatever*, explains to the narrator: "In the century of Louis XIV, [. . .] official culture placed the accent on the negation of pleasure and of the flesh; repeated insistently [. . .] that the only true source of happiness was in God. Such a discourse [. . .] would no longer be tolerated today. We need adventure and eroticism because we need to hear ourselves repeat that life is marvelous and exciting; and it's abundantly clear that we rather doubt this" (2011, 30).

In Houellebecq's novels, not only are we confronted with the social and psychological consequences of religion's decline, but we are also told that the decline is irreversible. All changes in social values turn out to be irreparable, as Daniel25 declares in *Possibility* apropos of the rise of Elohimism and the collapse of Islam and Christianity: "When a social system is destroyed, this destruction is definitive, and there can be no going back; the laws of social entropy, valid in theory for any human-relational system [. . .] had already, for a long time, been understood intuitively" (247–48). In the case of religion, materialism has destroyed the legend of the creator God, but surpassing materialism will depend not on a return to traditional religion, but on the surpassing of humanity itself. "The establishment of physical immortality," Houellebecq writes in "Positivist Preliminaries," "by means belonging to technology is without a doubt the necessary step to once again make religion possible" (2009, 252–53, my translation).

Where does this vision of religiosity in Houellebecq's novels come from? Is it a credible depiction of prevailing mentalities among Europeans? In fact, Houellebecq entertains in fictional form the advanced stages of an intellectual dogma known as classical secularization theory—the claim that with modernity comes the decay and disappearance of religion. Peter Berger, one of the most important modern proponents of secularization theory, writes in his 1967 book, *The Sacred Canopy*,

> By secularization we mean the process by which sectors of society and culture are removed from the domination of religious institutions and symbols. When we speak of society and institutions in modern Western history, of course, secularization manifests itself in the evacuation by the Christian churches of areas previously under their control or influence—as in the separation of church and state, or in the expropriation of church lands, or in the emancipation of education from ecclesiastical authority. When we speak of culture and symbols, however, we imply that secularization is more than a social-structural process. It affects the totality of cultural life and of ideation, and may be observed in the decline of religious contents in the arts, in philosophy, in literature, and, most important of all, in the rise of science as an autonomous, thoroughly secular perspective on the world. Moreover, it is implied here that the process of secularization has a subjective side as well. As there is a secularization of society and culture, so there is a secularization of consciousness. (105)

Secularization theory was a cornerstone of sociological thought for much of the nineteenth and twentieth centuries, but in recent decades numerous scholars have argued that its principal contention—that modernity and religion are mutually exclusive, the former leading to the demise of the latter—is not only inadequate to describe current trends in Western religiosity, but on some accounts may simply be mistaken.[5] Evidence for the theory's failure is, moreover, entirely empirical: religion simply *persists* in spite of modernity (see European Commission 2005). Contemporary reformulations of secularization theory have tried to place the emphasis not on the decline of religious belief but rather on the decline of the authority of religious institutions (see Chaves 1994), but the question that is unanswered in such analysis is whether, despite a decline in the social or political importance of religion, people are less pious, spiritual, or religious than they were in the past. From the perspective of many scholars, and in view of certain empirical data, the answer is a clear no.

Despite these modern reappraisals, Houellebecq's novels seem to insist that religion cannot survive, and indeed has not survived, the onslaught of modernity and the rationalizing and bureaucratizing forces unleashed by industrialization and the scientific revolution. As Desplechin explains in *The Elementary Particles*, "The West has sacrificed everything to this need [for rational certainty]: religion, happiness, hope—and, finally, its own life" (221). Houellebecq's novels do not, however, categorically celebrate the demise of religion, even if they often treat faith and spirituality with a considerable degree of contempt. As Douglas Morrey (2013, 114–51) has made clear, Houellebecq's novels retain a kind of vestigial nostalgia for religion and its psychosocial utility, and it may be for this reason that Houellebecq has been so keen to imagine quasi- or pseudo-religious alternatives (i.e., cloning cults) that could take the place of Christianity in a thoroughly secularized twenty-first-century Europe. Informed and perhaps inspired by Auguste Comte's views about religion's social function, Houellebecq has suggested that something in the religious vision of the world is necessary if civilization is to prosper. As Djerzinski muses to himself in *Particles*, "How could society function without religion [. . .]. It seemed difficult enough for an ordinary human being. For several days he studied the radiator beside his bed. It was a useful and ingenious device—when it was cold, the pipes filled with hot water—but how long could Western civilization continue without some kind of religion?" (135). Houellebecq has expressed this point of view in his nonfiction as well; he writes to Lévy, "Obviously, it is impossible for me to *establish* that for a society to cut itself off from the religious is tantamount to suicide; it is simply an intuition, but a persistent intuition" (2011, 161).

Houellebecq's intuition is not unfounded, and his novels—*The Elementary Particles* and *The Possibility of an Island* in particular—address what is an undeniable fact about many European countries: the importance of Christianity as an institution that structures social existence has waned dramatically. In France, for example, only 12.3 percent of French men and women attend church once or more per month, while in the United States the figure is 61.1 percent (Pfaff 2008). Sociologists of religion do not agree, however, on how to interpret this decline in religious practice, and their debates tend to center on precisely how the concept of secularization is to be understood. Does the secularization of Europe simply mean the faltering of religious institutions' political authority and influence on social organization? Does it denote the disappearance of overtly religious behavior, such as church attendance or having children baptized? Or is it rather the erosion of privately held belief, followed by the loss of individual faith?[6] These discussions have taken on a considerable degree of nuance in recent decades, but in Houellebecq's fiction the classical version of secularization theory is somewhat monolithically maintained, with secularization understood to function at every level of human reality. Houellebecq's novels tell the tale of religious decline from the viewpoint of total secularization—at once private, institutional, and political—in which the onset of modernity brings about the disappearance of religion *tout court*. In his early essay "Approches du désarroi," Houellebecq writes,

> The death of God in the West constituted the prelude to a tremendous metaphysical soap opera, which continues to this day. Any cultural historian would be able to piece together the details of the process: let us say in summary that Christianity was able to pull off this *masterstroke* of combining fierce belief in the individual [. . .] with the promise of eternal participation in the absolute Being. The dream having vanished, various attempts were made to promise the individual a minimum of being; to reconcile the dream of being that he carried within himself with the obsessive omnipresence of the future. At present, all these attempts have failed, and sorrow has continued to spread. (2009, 41, my translation)

Below, I explore how this view of contemporary European religiosity finds life in Houellebecq's novels. I also suggest that, despite the problems of the classical secularization model, the secularizing ethos of Houellebecq's fiction should be understood not as bad sociology but rather as a kind of experiment in the death of God, wherein characters experience predictable outcomes—the most frequent of which is suicide—based on their metaphysical assumptions.

Materialism and Suicide: Logical Consequences of the Death of God

Houellebecq's novels track the demise of a moribund West whose hedonistic preoccupations and irreligious ethos have pushed civilization to the brink of extinction. While *The Elementary Particles* deals specifically with the ways in which materialism has ravaged the lives of two characters—half brothers Bruno and Michel—the later work *The Possibility of an Island* speculates on the future of religion in the West and depicts the birth and rise of Elohimism, a new religious movement that supplants European Christianity and goes on to vanquish Islam and the other world faith traditions. Of particular interest in regard to the victory of materialism portrayed in Houellebecq's novels is their persistent representation of suicide. Confronted with aging, ugliness, chronic sexual dissatisfaction, or an obsessive and brooding disgust about humanity, characters both major and minor in Houellebecq's fiction have few ethical qualms about putting an end to their lives. The willingness to commit suicide on the part of many of Houellebecq's characters constitutes a litmus test for the demise of the Christian worldview and the concomitant spread of materialist ontology, for it is always—or nearly always—the case for Houellebecq's suicides that the calculation involved in self-slaughter only involves a reckoning about the prevention of pain. There is no consideration of the moral or theological connotations of suicide. With God absent from the Houellebecquian text, the divine prohibition on suicide is lifted. I focus below on the suicides in *The Elementary Particles* and on the euthanizing of Jed Martin's father in *The Map and the Territory*, since they present, to my mind, the most telling examples.

Houellebecq's award-winning second novel, *The Elementary Particles*, which appeared in 1998, tells the story of the half brothers Bruno and Michel, one a sex-obsessed, embittered high school literature teacher, the other a depressive, self-absorbed biophysicist, whose lives unravel as they enter middle age. Bruno and Michel are the sons of Janine Ceccaldi, an aging libertine who abandoned both children to their respective grandmothers in order to pursue a life of sexual freedom. Janine's negligence in caring for her children is truly disturbing: "Pushing open the door of one of the upstairs bedrooms, he [Marc Djerzinski, Michel's father] smelled a retch-inducing stench. The sun flared violently through the huge bay window onto the black and white tiles where his son crawled around awkwardly, slipping occasionally in pools of urine or excrement [. . .]. Sensing a human presence, the boy tried to escape; when Marc picked him up, the child trembled in his arms"

(2000a, 24). Forcibly removed from his mother's care, Michel is sent to live with his paternal grandmother in the Yonne, while the four-year-old Bruno ends up with Janine's mother in a low-rent apartment in Marseilles, where the old woman begins to go insane:

> [Bruno] remembered his grandmother, sitting on a suitcase in the middle of the kitchen on the day they arrived in Marseilles. Cockroaches scuttled between the cracks in the tiles. It was probably then that she began to lose her mind. The litany of troubles in those few short weeks had overwhelmed her: the slow agony of her husband's death, the hurried departure from Algiers and the arduous search for an apartment, finding one at last in a filthy housing project in the northeast of Marseilles. She had never set foot in France before. Her daughter had deserted her, and hadn't even attended her father's funeral. Deep down, Bruno's grandmother felt certain there had been a mistake. Someone, somewhere, had made a dreadful mistake. (32)

Bruno and Michel are both marked by their mother's abandonment, with Michel opting to avoid relationships with women altogether and Bruno sublimating his dereliction in the form of sexual obsessions.

An unattractive, forty-something divorcé who rarely sees his son, Bruno is a frequenter of nudist resorts, New Age camps, and sex colonies. Finally removed from his post as a teacher after coming on to a student, Bruno is reassigned as an administrator and divorces his wife, Anne, with whom he has a son named Victor. During a holiday at the Lieu du Changement—a sort of New Age colony where sexually frustrated forty-year-olds go to fornicate with strangers—Bruno meets Christiane, also an aging libertine (a *soixante-huitarde*, as she calls herself, referring to her sympathies for the student revolts of 1968), whom he begins to date seriously. Bruno is so focused on his sexual satisfaction with Christiane that everything else in his life, including his work and his son, ceases to have any meaning: "His colleagues, the thought-provoking seminars, the social development of the adolescent, multiculturalism . . . none of it had the slightest importance for him anymore. Christiane sucked his cock and looked after him when he was ill; Christiane was important. At that moment, he knew he would never see his son again" (198). However, when Christiane, who suffers from spinal necrosis, is paralyzed from the waist down in a macabre swingers club accident, Bruno hesitates in offering to take care of his now sexually nonfunctional lover, leading to Christiane's suicide:

> He had hesitated a couple of seconds too long: poor Christiane. Then he had hesitated a couple of days too long before calling her; he knew she was alone in her low-income apartment with her son [. . .]. There was nothing forcing him to look after a cripple, that's what she'd said, and he knew that she hadn't died hating him. Her broken wheelchair had been found at the bottom of the stairs near the mailbox. Her face was swollen and her neck broken. Bruno's name was on a form in the box marked "in the event of an accident, please contact . . ." She had died on the way to the hospital. (205)

Wracked by guilt after Christiane's death, Bruno commits himself to life in a mental institution, where a regimen of lithium and other psychotropic drugs effectively castrates him. However, even medication is not enough to quiet Bruno's sexual obsessions. As he says to Michel while on a short leave from the hospital to bury the two men's mother: "They've got me on lithium. [. . .] I'm not going back to the clinic just yet. I've got another night left. I'm going to a whorehouse [. . .]. Since they put me on lithium I can't get it up at all, but that doesn't matter, I'd still like to go" (216).

Michel, on the other hand, is a brilliant but deeply alienated biophysicist who lives his life at a distance from other human beings. Michel has avoided serious relationships all his life, but when at age forty he crosses paths with his high school sweetheart, Annabelle, the two begin dating and she becomes pregnant. Annabelle is an exceptionally beautiful woman who has paradoxically had little success with men. She tells Michel one evening after dinner:

> I haven't really had a happy life [. . .]. I think I was too obsessed with love. I fell for guys too easily; once they got what they wanted, they dumped me and I got hurt [. . .]. In the end, even the sex started to disgust me; I couldn't stand their triumphant little smiles when I took off my dress, or their idiot leers when they came and especially their boorishness once it was all over and done. They were spineless, pathetic and pretentious. In the end, it was too painful to know they thought of me as just another piece of meat. (192)

Sadly, soon after the pregnancy is discovered, Annabelle is diagnosed with uterine cancer, which quickly spreads to her intestine: "On 25 August, a routine examination revealed metastases in the abdomen [. . .]. Radiation therapy was a possibility—in fact, it was the only possibility—but it was important to realize that it was an arduous treatment and the chances of success were only fifty percent" (230). Preferring to avoid a painful and likely futile course of treatment, Annabelle takes her life by overdosing on painkillers, leaving her family in a state of incomprehension. "I don't understand," says Annabelle's mother. "I don't understand how life can be like this. She was a lovely girl, you know, always very affectionate, she never gave me any trouble. She never complained, but I knew she wasn't happy. She deserved better from life" (234). After Annabelle's death, Michel, heartbroken yet strangely composed, leaves France to pursue his research in Ireland, where after a period of ten years he makes discoveries in genetics that will soon allow the human race to replace itself with a species of immortal and asexual clones:

> At the end of 2009 there could no longer be any doubt: Djerzinski's conclusions were valid and could be considered to have been proven. The practical consequences were dizzying: any genetic code, however complex, could be noted in a standard, structurally stable form, isolated from disturbances or mutations. This meant that every cell contained within it the possibility of being infinitely copied. Every animal species, however highly evolved, could be transformed into a similar species reproduced by cloning, and immortal. (258)

At the novel's end, the narrator, whom Houellebecq reveals to be one of the future clones, praises the human race for its perseverance despite itself and dedicates the story of Bruno and Michel to a now nearly extinct mankind: "As the last members of this race are extinguished, we think it just to render this last tribute to humanity, an homage which itself will one day disappear, buried beneath the sands of time. It is necessary that this tribute be made, if only once. This book is dedicated to mankind" (264).

Bruno's and Michel's tragedies run deeper than the losses of their lovers and their mother's poor parenting. Houellebecq is not an author who is satisfied with solely psychological descriptions; his characters are as much the symptoms of broad cultural and historical tendencies as they are individual agents responsible for their own suffering: "Was it possible to think of Bruno as an individual? The decay of his organs was particular to him, and he would suffer his decline and death as an individual. On the other hand, his hedonistic worldview and the forces that shaped his consciousness and desires were common to an entire generation [. . .]. His motives, values and desires did not distinguish him from his contemporaries in any way" (148). Bruno's egotism, his lovers' fates, and his mother's negligence are superficial causes of his malaise; his ultimate undoing lies in his unwitting subjugation to the prevailing materialism of his time. In Bruno's view, the loss of belief in immortality lies at the root of religion's decline in Western civilization, and subsequently it has given rise to a cult of youth in which he, now middle-aged, is forbidden to participate. During the trip to their mother's deathbed in southern France, Bruno explains to Michel, "As soon as people stop believing in life after death, religion is impossible. If society is impossible without religion [. . .] then society isn't possible either [. . .]. Man has always been terrified by death—he's never been able to face the idea of his own disappearance [. . .] without horror. Of all worldly goods, youth is clearly the most precious, and today we don't believe in anything but worldly goods" (212–13).

Aware of the depravity and wickedness of his world, Bruno does nothing to change it. Rather, he wallows in his own dissipation, and in the end he fails to understand why his life has been destroyed. After Christiane's suicide, we read, "He knew his life was over, but he didn't understand the ending" (206). Rather than commit suicide, Bruno is institutionalized, and the last the reader sees of him is at his mother's death, when he promises to urinate on her ashes every day (211). Michel, meanwhile, manages to avoid insanity, though he makes a quick exit from life once his work is complete. Djerzinski is a man for whom being itself is a burden; as soon as he has left instructions for how the species is to put an end to its torment, he hurls himself into the sea. Speaking on behalf of the new race of clones, the narrator of the novel explains, "We now believe that Michel Djerzinski died in Ireland [. . .]. We also believe that, having completed his work, and with no human ties to bind him, he chose to die. Many witnesses attest to his fascination with this distant edge of the Western world [. . .] where, as he wrote, 'the sky, the sea and the light converge.' We now believe that Michel Djerzinski went into the sea" (253).

The number of suicides in *Particles* is one of the most memorable and troubling aspects of the text. The death of Annick, Bruno's first adolescent fling, whom Houellebecq describes as "not very pretty" and as someone whom Bruno "would have been embarrassed to be seen with [. . .] on the street" (127), is a particularly gruesome example of a suicide committed out of loathing for one's own body:

> Two policemen were trying to disperse a small crowd gathered outside Annick's building. Bruno went a little closer. The girl's body lay smashed and strangely twisted on the sidewalk. Her shattered arms seemed to form two strange limbs around her head. Her face, or what was left of it, lay in a pool of blood [. . .]. At that moment an ambulance arrived and two men got out carrying a stretcher. As they lifted her body he saw her shattered skull and turned away. The ambulance drove off in a howl of sirens. So ended Bruno's first love. (128)

Houellebecq's second novel is suicidal ideation pushed to the extreme. Not only are there the deaths of Michel, Annabelle, Christiane, and Annick, but there is also the outright, consensual eradication of the human race and its replacement by an improved species: "It has been surprising to note the meekness, resignation, perhaps even secret relief with which humans have consented to their own passing" (263). Annabelle's self-justification for administering herself a lethal dose of painkillers is exemplary of the prevailing mentality in the novel: "her body had taken a turn which was unfair and unexpected, and now could no longer be a source of joy or pleasure. On the contrary, it would gradually but quite quickly become another source of pain and embarrassment to her and others. And so she would have to destroy her body" (231). Annabelle offers one of Houellebecq's clearest demonstrations of materialism's inexorable logic: there is only the body, and reason dictates that once the body can no longer be counted on to provide pleasure, it is to be abandoned. The great injustice in the Houellebecquian universe is not sexual inequality, maternal abandonment, or capitalism; the great injustice in these novels is *matter*, and without recourse to the promise of the immaterial—the soul, God, eternity—the injustice is final.

The "sinfulness" of suicide lies in the person's disregard of divine will: God has a plan for human life and determines the moment of death for each of us, and trespassing against the Almighty in this respect risks everlasting damnation, or at best an extended stay in purgatory (for Catholics, at least). In *Particles*, however, the divine prohibition on suicide is a historical curiosity not unlike other anachronistic theological prohibitions on "sinful" behavior such as fornication or blasphemy. Whether to live or die is, at least theologically speaking, purely an individual matter, and what determines that choice is the state of the body. Where the body suffers, life is worthless; where the body rejoices, life is worthwhile. Suicide for Houellebecq's characters is simply a remedy for what they perceive to be needless suffering; any consideration of its sinfulness is almost shockingly absent.

The decision of Jed Martin's father in *The Map and the Territory* to be euthanized provides something of an apology for this secular rendering of suicide. Jean-Pierre Martin, who has had a highly successful career as an architect but is now afflicted with cancer and living in a nursing home, conveys to his son during a visit, "What [Jed] had to get into his head was that he could no longer be all right *anywhere*, that he couldn't be all right *in life generally* [. . .]. If he was going to keep on going they would have to change his artificial anus; well, he thought he'd had enough of that joke. And what's more, he felt pain. He couldn't bear it any longer, he was suffering too much" (2012, 217). Not long after Jed's visit, Jean-Pierre goes to Zurich to be euthanized at the hands of a for-profit assisted suicide venture called Koestler, which charges five thousand euros per lethal injection of pentobarbital sodium. Surprisingly, in *The Map and the Territory* Houellebecq mounts a stunning show of opposition to euthanasia in the person of Jed, who after meeting with the doctor who has overseen his father's suicide brutally attacks her in her office:

> The woman took back the file, obviously thinking their conversation was over, and got up to put it away in the filing cabinet. Jed stood up as well, approached, and slapped her violently. She made a stifled moan, but didn't have time to consider a riposte. He moved on to a violent uppercut to the chin, followed by a series of sharp cuffs. While she wavered on her feet, trying to get her breath back, he stepped back so as to kick her with all his strength at the level of her solar plexus. At this she collapsed to the ground, striking a metal corner of the desk as she fell; there was a loud cracking sound. The spine must have taken a blow, Jed thought. He leaned over her; she was groggy, breathing with difficulty, but she was breathing.[7] (240)

In Houellebecq's novels, the effort to alleviate human suffering has shifted from a more traditionally religious or Christian attempt to encourage sufferers to find meaning in their pain, to a focus on altering or simply eliminating the body so that suffering, both physical and mental, can be avoided as much as possible. Jean-Pierre's suicide (not to mention the creation of races of neohuman clones in *Particles* and *Possibility*) is the unsurprising consequence of this transformation, which despite Jed's protest still prevails in the ethical landscape of Western modernity in Houellebecq's fiction.

Materialism and suicide are causally linked in *Particles* and indirectly so in *The Map and the Territory*, with materialism providing the philosophical groundwork for the justification of suicide. With the divine prohibition on suicide lifted, it is only individual objectors like Jed who are left to mount an opposition to self-slaughter. Houellebecq's fiction presents a nexus of causality linking, on the one hand, secularization, materialism, and irreligion with, on the other hand, euthanasia and suicide (along with sexual liberation, free market economics, and a host of other modern ills). From a sociological point of view, something in this vision of terminal social decadence is surely exaggerated, but what Houellebecq's novels speak to, I suggest, in their mise-en-scène of secularization theory is not contemporary spiritual sentiment but rather the social and institutional decline of Europe's traditional religious institutions, French Catholicism in particular. By creating a universe of materialist horror in which suicide enjoys a broad cultural apology, materialism is the dominant worldview, and sexual freedom is nearly total, Houellebecq's novels are able to explore the consequences—in experimental form—of the decline of Catholic morality in French culture in the twentieth and twenty-first centuries.

Materialist Horror and Moral Secularization

A major advantage of contemporary reappraisals of secularization theory is that they have allowed scholars to avoid analyzing secularization as an all-or-nothing monolithic process whereby religiosity declines in every sense—from the political to the social to the personal. Rather, secularization can be viewed as a phenomenon that can operate on certain levels without necessarily operating on all of them. Social secularization may not augur or directly reflect secularization on a personal level, but it might be taken to indicate the emergence of a kind of "fuzzy fidelity" (see Voas 2009), where individual conviction suffers not from the internal pressure of private doubt but instead from the decollectivization of belief. By adapting

Houellebecq's portrayal of "post-religious" Europe to this conception of secularization, where the absence of a socially-structuring religious worldview, such as Catholicism in France, might harm the confidence or fervor associated with individual belief, the link between materialist horror and a genuine commentary on moral secularization and personal incredulity becomes discernible. Houellebecq's description of the priest Jean-Pierre Buvet's loss of faith in *Whatever* is a telling example of the fate of religion without a community context. Near the end of the novel, Buvet describes the collapse of his parish to the narrator:

> I'd told you Vitry wasn't an easy parish; it's even worse than you can imagine. Since my arrival I've tried to set up kids' groups; no kids ever came. It's three months now since I've celebrated a baptism. At mass I've never managed more than five people: four Africans and an old Breton woman; I believe she was eighty-two, an ex-employee of the railways. She'd been widowed for ages; her children didn't come to see her anymore, she no longer had their address. On Sunday I didn't see her at mass. I passed by her house, she lives in a high-priority housing area [. . .]. Her neighbors told me she'd just been attacked; they'd taken her off to hospital, but she only had slight fractures. I visited her; her fractures were taking time to mend, of course, but there was no danger. When I went back a week later she was dead. I asked for explanations, but the doctors refused to give me any. They'd already cremated her body; nobody in the family had bothered to attend. I'm certain she'd have wished for a religious burial; she hadn't said as much to me, she never spoke of death; but I'm certain that's what she'd have wanted. (138)

On the next page the reader learns that the doctors at the hospital have euthanized the old woman, whom they considered to be an "unnecessary burden" (139).

Interestingly, the young nurse who had administered the lethal dose comes to see Buvet in confession a few days later, claiming she is unable to sleep. Patricia, who "knew nothing about religious matters" (139), begins to visit Jean-Pierre nearly every night, and the two develop an affectionate though chaste relationship. Buvet is tempted to break his vows, but any hope of sleeping with Patricia evaporates when she announces she has begun seeing someone else. Buvet explains to the narrator, "She told me we wouldn't see each other again, but that she was glad to have known me; she really liked changing boyfriends; she was only twenty. Basically she liked me a lot; but no more than that; it was mainly the idea of sleeping with a priest that excited her" (140). Buvet gets drunk as he tells his story and expresses a reluctance to say mass the next morning: "Tomorrow I must say mass. I don't see how I can do it. I don't think I can cope. I no longer feel the presence" (140). The narrator responds by asking "what presence?" (140), but Buvet does not answer. The narrator calls a cab and leaves; Buvet does not reappear in the novel.

Buvet's loss of faith may say more about the state of Catholicism in France than it does about the fate of religion in the West. France's peculiar relationship with the Roman Catholic Church, marked by revolution, violence, and political upheaval, has contributed to an environment in which Catholicism, long associated with social privilege and political obscurantism, no longer appeals to most contemporary French men and women. The church's refusal to adopt basic elements of Western modernity (for instance, by forbidding Catholics to use condoms) does not help its chances in a country where the Catholic contestation of secular political authority was a cause of division and violence for centuries. Buvet's defunct parish is the result not so much of a general decline of religion, but rather of a slackening of the social significance of an increasingly obsolete and socially irrelevant Catholicism. In *The Map and the Territory*, Houellebecq confirms his account of the plight of the priesthood:

> Inheritors of a millennia-old spiritual tradition that nobody really understood anymore, once placed in the front rank of society, priests today were reduced, at the end of terrifyingly long and difficult studies that involved mastering Latin, canon law, rational theology, and other almost incomprehensible subjects, to surviving in miserable material conditions. They took the metro alongside other men, going from a Gospels-reading group to a literacy workshop, saying mass every morning for a thin and aging audience, being forbidden all sensual joy or even the elementary pleasures of family life, yet obliged by their function to display day after day an unwavering optimism [. . .]. Humble and penniless, sneered at by everyone, subjected to all the problems of urban life without having access to any of its pleasures, young urban priests constituted, for those who did not share their faith, a puzzling and inaccessible subject. (59)

Priests in Houellebecq's novels are a dying breed whose social utility appears to have run its course. They are historical anachronisms, anthropological curiosities whose presence on the Paris Metro is as uncanny as that of an escaped animal that wanders into a restaurant. Buvet's parish, it should be noted, lies in the suburban city of Vitry, a Parisian banlieue home to a large population of Muslims. The presence of a religious alternative in the community likely does not help matters for poor Buvet.[8]

Whatever is a novel that shows more than it tells. The reader is able to understand Buvet's spiritual collapse as a consequence of religious change—the decline of Catholicism in France—and his own personal experience, rather than as evidence of a more general decline of religious belief and sentiment among Westerners. The murder of his elderly parishioner, though certainly horrific, can be understood as an exaggerated rendering of moral secularization in a post-Christian or post-Catholic social and cultural context, rather than as the kind of materialist horror we find in the suicides of such characters as Annabelle, Djerzinski, and Daniel1. In this respect, then, it would be a mistake to go too far in reading Houellebecq as a sort of crypto-Catholic reactionary writer bent on proclaiming a return to traditional morality (see Lindenberg 2002, 23). Indeed, his subsequent novels, particularly *The Possibility of an Island* and *The Elementary Particles*, display such an overt embrace of classical accounts of secularization that one would have difficulty finding anything reactionary about them; rather, in these novels, the damage to traditional religion is total and irreversible, and there can be no going back to previous times.

Houellebecq admits to Lévy in *Public Enemies* that he found Catholicism compelling as a young man (2011, 137–38), perhaps even up to the point of writing *Whatever.* But from the appearance of *The Elementary Particles* until only very recently,[9] Houellebecq's tone was clearly one of thoroughgoing atheism. As Houellebecq states in his 2001 interview with *Lire*, "God doesn't exist, and even if you're stupid you end up realizing it." Since *Whatever*, then, Houellebecq has tended to generalize his atheism in his novels, with the effect that these texts stand as fictionalized accounts of theories of secularization that are themselves fictions. Characters such as Bruno and Michel Djerzinski are exaggerated and somewhat lampooned victims of the materialist worldview that Houellebecq's novels identify as typical of the age, and they offer gripping portrayals of a certain kind of contemporary mentality. But we should avoid the temptation to view such characters as exemplary of prevailing worldviews, and should instead understand them as particular variables in Houellebecq's materialist horror experiment. Houellebecq's novels provide morally compelling fables of the psychosocial horrors of materialism, which we should consider to be experimental explorations of the individual and collective psychological consequences of God's death and which we should avoid reducing to sociological documents.

With the social significance of Christianity having declined steeply in many European countries, it is legitimate to wonder if deinstitutionalized religious belief, of the sort found among many French men and women, will remain merely personal or if it will some day coalesce into more collective forms. Religious vacuums are historical oddities, and past efforts to forcibly secularize societies have not only failed but have also been responsible for a tremendous amount of bloodletting (as have been attempts to spiritualize societies). Is it possible, then, that the twenty-first century will see the rise of a new religion in the "post-Christian" West? *The Possibility of an Island* is concerned with just this question. I turn to this novel in the next chapter.

The Future of Religion

Political or military events, economic transformations, aesthetic or cultural mutations can all play a role, sometimes a very big role, in the life of men; but nothing, ever, can have any historical importance compared to the development of a new religion, or to the collapse of an existing one.

—**Houellebecq 2007**

But such a state of uncertainty and confused agitation cannot last forever. The day will come when our societies will know once again hours of creative effervescence, in the course of which new ideals will be born and new formulae emerge which will for a time serve as a guide to humanity.

—**Durkheim 1994**

One of the most provocative aspects of Houellebecq's fiction is its willingness to engage religion as a serious antidote to contemporary existential malaise. Long an atheist and now a self-identified agnostic, Houellebecq is nonetheless a deeply and unavoidably religious writer, and not to read his work *religiously* is to read it only partially, if not simply poorly. Just as he was for Comte, man for Houellebecq is an "animal of the religious type," and ignoring this dimension of human nature risks everything from individual destruction to social collapse. As Douglas Morrey has written, "If we are to avoid the kind of collective suicide that Houellebecq repeatedly envisions in his fiction, it may well require a solution with the organizational structure and the force of conviction of a religion" (2013, 151). On a similar note, if we are to avoid reading Houellebecq inaccurately, we must acknowledge that perhaps no other living French writer exhibits a comparable sensitivity to the psychological, social, and political stakes of religious change in France, if not in Europe and the West in general.

Morrey's insight finds notable confirmation in Houellebecq's fourth novel, *The Possibility of an Island*, which, structured much like the Bible,[1] tells the story of the Elohimite sect, a new religious movement that emerges in Western Europe at the beginning of the twenty-first century and attracts adherents with a promise of physical immortality through cloning. Miskiewicz, the scientific leader of the movement, describes the Elohimite version of immortality to a gathering of converts:

> The human being is matter plus information. The composition of this matter is now known to us, at least in principle: It is based entirely on DNA, that of the nucleus and that of the mitochondria [. . .]. Why not directly manufacture an adult human being, from the necessary chemical elements and the schema provided by the DNA? [. . .] The men of the future will be born directly into an adult body, a body aged eighteen, and this is the model that will be subsequently reproduced, it is in this ideal form that they will reach [. . .] immortality. (2007, 167)

In the course of the narrative, Elohimism grows to become the largest religion on the planet, and much of the movement's success relies on its ability to appeal to, rather than condemn, contemporary materialism. The religion favors euthanasia as a remedy to the "miseries" of old age and encourages total sexual freedom among its members; moreover, the Elohimites eschew supernatural reality and the existence of an immortal soul, preferring to limit "transcendence" to the immortalizing of the physical body and the transfer of neural information from one clone to the next. Daniel25, the twenty-fifth in a series of clones that begins with the novel's protagonist, Daniel1, explains, "[Elohimism] was adapted perfectly to the leisure civilization in which it had been born. Imposing no moral constraints [. . .] it did not hesitate [. . .] to make its own the fundamental promise at the core of all monotheistic religions: victory over death. Eradicating any spiritual or confusing dimension, it simply limited the scope of this victory [. . .] to the unlimited prolongation of material life" (248).

Elohimism's unswerving commitment to materialism reflects Houellebecq's fascination with the positivist philosophy of Auguste Comte. Religion in the Comtean view constitutes the central facilitator of social unity, and under ideal conditions it need not require any reference to supernatural entities at all. The only proper object of religious worship in Comte's system is society itself, condensed in all its myriad manifestations into the Great Being. Humanity is the only reality (Comte 1968, 334) and can stand in place of God both as a source of epistemological and moral authority and as a focus of veneration. Summarizing Comte's social understanding of the role of religion in "Préliminaires au positivisme," composed as an introduction to *Auguste Comte aujourd'hui* (Bourdeau et al. 2003), Houellebecq writes:

> Man belongs to a social species; this fact is at the foundation of Comte's thought, and we must never lose sight of it if we want to have a chance of understanding its evolution. In his examination of the human species' social formations, their various forms of organization, their future, Comte is almost exhaustive [. . .]. But of all the structures produced by a society, and which in turn form its basis, religion appears to him to be the most significant, the most characteristic, and the most threatened. Man, according to Comte, can more or less be defined as a social animal of the religious type. (2009, 251, my translation)

On the other hand, positivism maintains, if only implicitly, a doctrine of rigid mind-body physicalism. Recognizing the social importance of religion, though considering traditional beliefs in immortality to be "childish illusions" (Comte 1968, 347),[2] Comte attempts to elaborate a religion of humanity capable of unifying social life around reverence for the social body and the veneration of ancestors. Nonetheless, no provision is made in Comte's system for the human desire for immortality, other than an abstract notion of eternal life in the memory of human beings: "The noble emulation aroused by the continuous glorification of our predecessors will push everyone to merit [. . .] this irrevocable incorporation into the immense and eternal being [. . .]. The new public education will have soon inclined all positivists to feel, in such a reward for all honorable conduct, a full equivalent to the vain hopes that drove their precursors" (346). In other words, satisfaction with having contributed to the flourishing of the Great Being and with having emulated society's most honorable members is to be adequate compensation for the eternal life promised by Christianity, a doctrine that Comte identifies (falsely, as I suggested in chapter 1) as increasingly obsolete.

Houellebecq may share Comte's allegiance to mind-body physicalism, but he is profoundly skeptical that a religion without the supernatural—specifically, without the notion of an immortal soul—will ever be taken seriously. He writes,

> Comte had indeed recognized that the mission of religion was to unite humanity and to rule over its actions; he had planned the sacraments and the calendar. He had perhaps not grasped the depth of man's innate desire for immortality [. . .]. Abstract immortality inscribed in human memory nonetheless failed to convince his contemporaries—not to mention us—who were hungry for a promise of more material survival. Indeed, let us suppose that the prerequisites of Comte's system have been realized [. . .]. In what way will we have advanced [. . .] toward the establishment of a common religion? In what way will the notion of humanity, or of the Great Being, be more desirable to individuals? And what will be able to lead them, aware of their individual extinction, to be satisfied with participation in this theoretical fetish? Who, in the end, can be interested in a religion that does not make a guarantee against death? (2009, 251–52, my translation)

Elohimism proposes a solution to the inadequacies of Comte's religion of humanity, even as it upholds the basic tenets of the positivist view of religion. Elohimism not only unites its followers around a common hope for immortality, embellished by rituals and practices dedicated to affirming that hope, but, even more important, it is able to promise its members eternal life where Comte's religion of humanity cannot—though in this case without appeal to the supernatural. Through cloning, the immortality once thought to be the exclusive domain of immaterial transcendence can now be realized technologically: not only does the Elohimite Church store its followers' DNA, but it also pledges to transmit their memories to future clones by means of a "molecular transfer" (Houellebecq 2007, 27). Religion becomes possible when achieving immortality becomes a matter of scientific innovation. The positivist system of religion and the cult of the Great Being are only sustainable if the promise of personal immortality can be included in the package. Elohimism is able to offer such spiritual goods, though one naturally wonders what Comte, who claims that living for others constitutes the supreme form of happiness (1968, 353), would have thought about its unrestrained hedonism.

Houellebecq's portrayal of Elohimism also invokes questions about the definition of religion that go back to the very beginnings of sociology. In the classical Durkheimian (1994, 147) view, religion's two functions are to unite the social body and to explain the nature of reality; worship of and belief in supernatural entities is incidental to the worship of society, and thus it is possible to consider a wide variety of social movements as religious in form, even if they do not have supernatural qualities. Since Durkheim, however, various and often competing definitions of religion have emerged, some of which part ways significantly with Durkheim's original formulation. Rodney Stark (2004, 2), for example, has argued that Durkheim errs rather grievously in his exclusion of belief in the supernatural from the definition of religion. Other (perhaps less polemical) attempts to define religion prefer instead to avoid the notion of a singular "essence," proposing a series of dimensions or common characteristics that religions typically possess.[3] All religions might, for example, be expected to make provision for "solace in the face of suffering and death" (Benthall 2008, 22), to "appeal to supernatural entities" (40), or to provide "moral imperatives based on altruism" (44). More critical formulations, such as Talal Asad's (1993, 27–54), view religion as an anthropological category that was "disembedded" from a more holistic, unified polity as Western culture emerged from medievalism into modernity.[4] My goal in this chapter, in part, is to subject Elohimism to examination according to these various renderings of the definition of religion.

Finally, and perhaps most significantly, *The Possibility of an Island* raises serious questions about the future of religiosity in Western societies. Should we expect a fringe cult movement to rise up and supplant a decayed European Christianity? Is this fundamentally or necessarily inconceivable? Or, beginning from the premise that religious vacuums are historically much more the exception than the rule, should not such a possibility strike us as rather alarmingly plausible? I argue that *The Possibility of an Island* offers more than an exploration of religious change and innovation in a purportedly post-Christian Europe. Despite the anxieties the novel identifies (and at least seemingly tries to palliate) in the "secular" Western psyche, *Possibility* may also be read as a more subtle attempt on Houellebecq's part to imagine a religious alternative not to a defunct Christianity, but rather to a real and considerably more formidable competitor: Islam.

The Return of Religion

The Possibility of an Island is perhaps Houellebecq's most philosophically dense novel. It is only in this text that his criticism of materialist culture—and along with it the West's principal humanist alternatives to Christian civilization, socialism and liberalism—culminates in a sustained exploration of a religious solution to human suffering. The novel tells the story of two parallel historical developments in twenty-first-century Western civilization: the triumph of the cult of youth as the focus of a moral, political, and economic consensus, and the birth of a new religion, Elohimism, that panders to the prevailing materialism of the age. Caught up in the sweep of these transformations is Daniel, the novel's narrator, a sex-obsessed, aging comedian who has made a fortune thanks to his outrageously offensive sense of humor and calculated indifference to taboos.

The aesthetic values of Daniel's time are utterly debauched. The comedian's most successful sketch, "We Prefer the Palestinian Orgy Sluts" (33), achieves critical renown in an artistic environment in which morality has been put to death and where "[a]ny form of cruelty, cynical selfishness, or violence was therefore welcome—certain subjects, like parricide or cannibalism, in particular" (36). Houellebecq offers this description of the last comedy show of Daniel's career:

> Bizarrely entitled *Forwards Snowy! Onwards to Aden!*, my last show was subtitled "100% Hateful" [and . . .] it was in no way hyperbole. From the outset, I got onto the subject of the conflict in the Middle East [. . .] in a manner which, wrote the *Le Monde* journalist, was "singularly abrasive." The first sketch, entitled "The Battle of the Tiny Ones," portrayed Arabs—renamed Allah's vermin—Jews—described as "circumcised fleas"—and even some Lebanese Christians, afflicted with the pleasing sobriquet of "Crabs from the Cunt of Mary." [. . .] The rest of the show included a screamingly funny playlet entitled "The Palestinians Are Ridiculous," into which I slipped a variety of burlesque and salacious allusions about sticks

of dynamite that female militants of Hezbollah put around their waists in order to make mashed Jew. (41)

Early in the narrative, Daniel meets Isabelle, a beautiful woman in her late thirties who, like Daniel, has become rich by exploiting Western civilization's crumbling moral and religious foundations. The editor of a popular teen magazine called *Lolita*, Isabelle witnesses firsthand the desperation with which women thirty and older have begun to venerate the nubile flesh of adolescent girls: "More and more, mothers would tend to copy their daughters. Obviously there's something ridiculous about a thirty-year-old woman buying a magazine called *Lolita*; but no more so than her buying a clinging top, or hot pants. [. . .] the feeling of ridiculous [. . .] was going to gradually disappear and be replaced by pure fascination with limitless youth" (29). Isabelle acknowledges the ridiculousness of her magazine's clientele, even while she remains as obsessed as her readers with warding off the physical effects of aging. She and Daniel live happily in southern Spain for a number of years, but as Isabelle nears her fortieth birthday, she begins to despair at the sight of her body: "I [Daniel] could feel her, at the moment when I glanced at her, wincing slightly, as if she had felt a punch between the shoulder blades [. . .]. The beauty of her fine, sensitive face was of the kind that resists time; but her body [. . .] was beginning to suffer the first blows of age—blows which [. . .] were going to multiply rapidly, leading to total degradation" (38). Daniel does not love Isabelle any less for the decline of her beauty. But in lieu of making love, the two adopt a dog, Fox, who brings them joy despite the gnawing lack of tenderness between them.

Things do not improve, however, and while Daniel is away on vacation Isabelle goes on a physically catastrophic drinking binge. Afterward, disgusted by her body and unable to feel love, Isabelle leaves Daniel and returns to France: "She could no longer stand herself; and, consequently, she could no longer stand love, which seemed to her to be false" (50). Faced with his marriage's collapse, Daniel remarks, "The disappearance of tenderness always closely follows that of eroticism [. . .]. When physical love disappears, everything disappears; a dreary, depthless irritation fills the passing days. And, with regard to physical love, I hardly had any illusions. Youth, beauty, strength: the criteria for physical love are exactly the same as those of Nazism" (50–51).

Optimistically, one might read this passage as a protest on Daniel's part against the glorified youth culture that has been the source both of Isabelle's wealth and of her ruin. If, after all, what is required for physical love—and thus love generally—is a society of Nazis, perhaps Daniel will attempt to find some new basis for his relationship with Isabelle. But such an exercise in optimism would be out of character for Houellebecq. Daniel is indeed far from done with love—or to put things in more Houellebecquian terms, he is far from done with sex. Soon after Isabelle's departure, he meets the beautiful twenty-one-year-old Esther, a Spanish actress with whom he begins a wild, desperate, and ultimately destructive affair. Daniel says of her, "I will just say, without exaggeration or metaphor, that [Esther] gave life back to me. In her company, I lived moments of intense happiness. It was perhaps the first time I had had the opportunity to utter this simple sentence. I lived moments of intense happiness; inside her, or just next to her; when I was inside her, or just before, or just after" (119). Typical of Houellebecq's male protagonists, Daniel is unable to live according to his own principles: while he may recognize the materialist horror of contemporary culture (he has made a career doing precisely this), he still prefers a society of "Nazis" to preserving his marriage on grounds other than sex. He is some mixture of helpless animal and moral coward, incapable of overcoming the flesh that, as he knows all too well, will ultimately ruin him.

At forty-seven, Daniel is terrified that Esther will abandon him for a younger man. He spends what time he can with her in Madrid, where she lives with her much older sister, and when back home at his residence in Andalusia he waits frantically for Esther to return his phone calls. The affair drags on, and though Daniel experiences moments of intense happiness with her (though it is happiness of a mostly sexual nature), he knows deep down that this relationship, which is bound to end when Esther finds someone her own age, is going to be his undoing: "love makes you weak, and the weaker of the two is oppressed, tortured, and finally killed by the other, who in his or her turn oppresses, tortures, and kills without having evil intentions, without even getting pleasure from it, with complete indifference; that's what men, normally, call love" (130). Esther is a creature well suited to the materialistic, hedonistic twenty-first-century European environment of *Possibility*. She refuses to kiss Daniel: like many of the young people of her generation, she does not have a great interest in love, while she certainly has a tremendous penchant for sex. Daniel "loves" Esther, Houellebecq assures us, but Daniel is too old to be naïve about the sort of person she is:

> Esther was certainly not *well educated* in the normal sense of the term, the thought never crossed her mind to empty an ashtray, or

to clear away what was left on her plate, and she didn't mind in the slightest about leaving the lights on behind her in the rooms she had just left; there was also no question of asking her to think of doing the shopping, to bring anything back from a shop that was not intended for her own use, or more generally to do any kind of favor for anyone. Like all very pretty young girls she was basically only good for fucking, and it would have been stupid to employ her for anything else. (152)

Esther is, Daniel says, a "little animal, who [is] innocent, amoral, neither good nor evil, who [is] simply in search of her ration of excitement and pleasure" (234). It is therefore no surprise that, offered an acting job in New York, Esther rather flippantly abandons Daniel, humiliating him on the eve of her departure during a party she throws in Madrid for her twenty-third birthday. It is at this party that Daniel is directly confronted with Esther's frivolity and, by extension, her infidelity:

I realized I hadn't caught sight of Esther for some time, and I began vaguely to search for her [. . .]. In the end I discovered her in one of the far bedrooms, stretched out in the middle of a group; she had taken off most of her clothes [. . .]. A boy lying behind her [. . .] was caressing her ass, and readying himself to penetrate her. She was speaking to another boy [. . .] whom I didn't recognize; at the same time, she was playing with his sex, tapping it against her nose and her cheeks and smiling all the while. I closed the door discreetly; I didn't know it yet, but this was to be the last image I would keep of her. (237)

Abandoned by his capricious lover, Daniel tends slowly toward suicide, having declared, "All energy is of a sexual nature, not mainly, but exclusively, and when the animal is no longer good for reproducing, it is absolutely no longer good for anything; it is the same for men" (154). Daniel is a man whose principal concern in life has been with being able to get and maintain an erection; he has never made any real distinction between happiness and sex; and a sense of purpose outside of his carnal predilections is utterly absent. After discovering Esther fornicating with her friends, Daniel's dejection is so total that he masturbates in public, a desperate attempt to call attention to his threatened virility: "Later still, as dawn was breaking on Madrid, I masturbated quickly near the pool. A few meters away from me there was a girl dressed in black, with a vacant look in her eyes; I thought she wouldn't even notice my presence, but she spat to one side when I ejaculated" (237). Terrified by physical aging, decline, and the prospect of abandonment, while at the same time unable to console himself with even the vaguest notion of an ultimate purpose, Daniel is one more casualty in Houellebecq's catalog of the victims of materialism. His suicidal thoughts come as no surprise: "He wallowed in humiliation, and in the most abject manner possible. He went as far as offering [Esther] money, lots of money, just to spend a last night with her [. . .]. She had even thought of contacting the police, but he just hung around the area [. . .] and finally he disappeared" (298).

During the course of this appalling commentary on the fate of the old—or, more precisely, the not-young—in a culture where youth has become the ultimate and unquestionable good, the reader encounters the Elohimites, a group of New Age religious practitioners who believe life was brought to earth by extraterrestrials and who place their hope for immortality in the prospect of cloning. Elohimism is well adapted to the prevailing materialism of the day: basing its entire appeal on the promise of physical immortality, the cult offers its members an eternity of health and pleasure, free from any confusing spiritual or metaphysical considerations:

> More and more, men were going to want to live freely, irresponsibly, on a wild quest for pleasure; they were going to want to live like those who were already living among them, the *kids*, and when old age would make its weight felt, when it would become impossible for them to continue to struggle, they would put an end to it all; but in the meantime they would have joined the Elohimite Church, their genetic code would have been safeguarded, and they would die in the hope of an indefinite continuation of that same existence that was devoted to pleasure. (291)

The Elohimites' desire is to live as perpetual Esthers, pursuing physical gratification without any fear of abandonment or consequence, while avoiding the fate of Daniel and Isabelle, who can no longer continue to struggle and will disappear forever with the death of their bodies. Elohimism represents a solution to the problem of aging that the novel poses, but that solution is nothing if not radical: we waste our time trying to reconcile ourselves to death; it is better simply to overcome it, by whatever means necessary.

Elohimism is a resounding success in the secular, post-Christian West of *The Possibility of an Island.* While it draws many of its initial members from the "atheistic, well-off, modern milieus" (283), the Elohimite Church quickly becomes the dominant religion of Europe and then of the entire world, even managing to overwhelm Islam. The clones of the church's original members, who appear at the beginning of the text, have survived a series of wars and natural disasters, and they lead solitary lives inside heavily fortified compounds, which have been built to protect them from the few "human savages" that remain at the beginning of the fifth millennium. The neohuman clones have kept detailed records of their human predecessors, and the picture they paint of the last years of human civilization is shocking. Daniel25—the twenty-fifth incarnation of the original Daniel—writes of old age in Daniel1's time, "In the years preceding the disappearance of the species, [old age] had manifestly become atrocious to the point where the level of voluntary deaths, prudishly renamed *departures* [. . .] was nearing 100 percent, and the average age of departure [. . .] was falling toward fifty in the most developed countries" (62). Following a tradition begun by Daniel1, each clone is required to produce a "life story" for his or her subsequent incarnation: according to Daniel25, the life stories of the original members agree without exception on the "unbearable nature of the mental suffering caused by old age" (62). While, in the text, events such as the massive dying-off of elderly men and women during a 2003 European heat wave manage at first to provoke the "obligatory indignation," Daniel24 explains that this indignation "quickly faded, and the development of active euthanasia—or, increasingly often, active voluntary euthanasia—would, in the course of the following decades, solve the problem" (63).

Such criminal disregard for the happiness and suffering of the old, who, unable to participate in the culture of youth, come progressively to be treated "purely as rubbish" (63), would be "inconceivable in Africa, or in a traditional Asian country" (63), where ancestors are venerated. But in "an authentically modern country" (63), such as France, scenes similar to what occurred in the summer of 2003 are characteristic:

> More than ten thousand people [. . .] had died in the country; some had died alone in their apartments, others in the hospital or in retirement homes, but all had essentially died because of a lack of care. In the weeks that followed, [*Libération*] published a series of atrocious reports [. . .] relating the agony of old people crammed

> into communal rooms, naked on their beds, in diapers, moaning all day without anyone coming to rehydrate them or even to give them a glass of water; describing the rounds made by nurses unable to contact the families who were on vacation, regularly gathering up the corpses to make space for new arrivals. (62–63)

Elohimism makes the repetition of these gruesome scenes unnecessary. Fear of death need not force one to cling foolishly to a decrepit life: the Elohimite wisely relinquishes the body once it becomes a source of suffering and awaits reincarnation in a new, youthful form. Though primarily a cult of youth, Elohimism is also a cult of death: promoting the elimination of physical undesirables, the religion provides moral justification for ridding society of its older members, whose physical appearance has become a source of terror and disgust for the young and whose care requirements interfere with the life of carefree pleasure that twenty-first-century Westerners have come to expect.

The rise of the Elohimite Church confirms a thesis that Houellebecq has been developing throughout his work: Western civilization, for lack of any reference to an ultimate principle that might found some sense of social unity and satisfy the human desire for immortality, is reverting to barbarism. The extermination of the old is the final stage of the process: for the first time in history, aging humans are consenting en masse to their own extinction, while the younger generation, à la Esther, participates in more and more superficial and bestial forms of pleasure. The similarities between Daniel25's description of the "savages" of the fifth millennium and Western culture in the twenty-first century in *Possibility* are exemplary in this regard. Daniel25 recounts a fight between two older members of a tribe wandering in a post-apocalyptic Spain:

> At first the fight took place in the utmost silence; but from the first sight of blood the savages began to shout and whistle to encourage the antagonists. I understood immediately that it would be a fight to the death, with the aim of eliminating the individual least able to survive; the combatants struck each other without inhibition, trying to reach the face or other sensitive parts of the body [. . .]. The most corpulent one seemed in difficulty, he had lost a lot of blood [. . .]. [He] staggered to his feet; without wasting a second, his adversary leaped onto him and plunged his dagger into his eye. He fell

> to the ground, his face spattered with blood, and the scramble for the spoils began. With lifted daggers, the males and females of the tribe threw themselves screaming onto the wounded man [. . .]. At first they cut off bits of flesh that they roasted in the embers, but as the frenzy increased they began to devour the body of the victim directly [. . .]. I supposed that it was a rite of union, a way of strengthening bonds in the group—at the same time as eliminating weakened or sick members; *all of this seemed to conform to what I had been taught about mankind.* (320–21, my emphasis)

The verdict in *The Possibility of an Island* leaves little room for ambiguity: materialism leads not simply to nihilism, despair, and suicide—this much was already apparent in *The Elementary Particles*—but, in the end, materialism results in the reanimalization of the human species. In the face of this final degradation, Elohimism represents a last-ditch effort to preserve some minimum of humanity, if only by staving off the animal terror of extinction. At the same time, it fully acquiesces to the bestial, pleasure-seeking worldview that has become typical of the age.

Can a Cloning Cult Be a Religion?

The Elohimite Church unites its adherents around a simple proposition: God may be dead, and with him the soul, but technology, through the process of cloning, grants people the possibility of at least some minimal transcendence. Is this singular emphasis on immortality enough to make Elohimism a religion? As I discussed above, a consensus on the definition of religion has historically eluded scholars, with the debate often centering on the degree to which belief in the supernatural should be included in the definition. In other cases—such as the debate between Geertz and Asad—the issue has been to determine whether religion is simply a recent anthropological category, which only became distinct *as religion* when practices today deemed to be "religious" became disembedded from other cultural institutions. Below, I subject Elohimism to analysis under several criteria, including the traditional concept of *religare*, or "binding," of both man to man and man to God; Durkheim's classical distinction between the sacred and the profane; belief in the supernatural; and the interpretation of religion as a recently disembedded (and largely Christian) anthropological category. Elohimism fits comfortably into the first two conceptions of religion, but its materialistic foundations make it difficult, though not impossible, to identify the movement as a religion within a supernatural paradigm. Additionally, it is possible to interpret both the decline of Christianity charted in *The Elementary Particles* and the rise of Elohimism in *Possibility* as a mise-en-scène of the Asadian model—that is, an attempt to embed (or reembed) religion within a total cultural system, where identification of the political, the religious, the economic, and so on as distinct and separate spheres is no longer appropriate or even intelligible.

Religion as religare. The origins of the word "religion" are obscure, but it has been common for scholars to interpret the combination of the Latin prefix *re-* and the verb *ligare* as conveying the notion of rebinding, in particular of humans to God through the person of Christ. The notion can also be extrapolated beyond its theological denotation to connote a binding of people to each other under the auspices of a shared faith, or "in" the body of Christ, whose dual human and divine status permits both a vertical and a horizontal integration of the human being into ultimate reality, both divine and social. In a more contemporary context, the rebinding power of religion can be viewed as an alternative to the atomizing forces of modernity that haunt Houellebecq's fiction, with Elohimism providing a system of belief and practice that fosters human unity amid the destruction that unchecked individualism has wrought.

In the specific case of *Possibility*, Houellebecq has created a fictionalized twenty-first-century Europe in which Christianity has succumbed to consumerism and the cult of youth; the old are treated as human refuse and left to die alone in hospitals and retirement homes; and mainstream art glamorizes cruelty, egotism, and violence. Even the human ability to love has not survived in the age of materialism. Daniel1's description of Esther and her friends reveals the extent of the destruction:

> What I was feeling, these young people could not feel, nor even exactly understand, and if they had been able to feel something like it, it would have made them uncomfortable [. . .]. They had succeeded, after decades of conditioning and effort, they had finally succeeded in tearing from their hearts one of the oldest human feelings, and now it was done, what had been destroyed could no longer be put back together, no more than the pieces of a broken cup can be reassembled, they had reached their goal: at no moment in their lives would they ever know love. They were free. (236)

In this terrifying future, where deep, loving human relationships have become not so much impossible as simply unwanted, traditional forms of human collectivity have been abandoned. Where once, in the Houellebecquian vision, Christianity succeeded in uniting humanity under a shared moral code, in the twenty-first century of *Possibility* mankind's sole moral imperative has become to pursue pleasure at all costs and, once the body can no longer support such pursuits, to exit existence altogether.

Elohimism, however, by unifying humanity around a common hope for immortality, does at least produce a semblance of shared moral order, even if it appears flagrantly antihumanistic: the leaders of the Elohimite Church, in promising immortality to their adherents, believe, much as Djerzinski does in *The Elementary Particles*, that through technology they can restore the conditions that make love possible. Vincent, the prophet of the Elohimite Church, tells Daniel1, "Man has never been able to love, apart from in immortality; it is undoubtedly why women were closer to love when their mission was to give life. We have discovered immortality. [. . .] the world no longer has the power to destroy us, it is we, rather, who have the power to create" (286). Elohimism fulfills the social sense of religare: it binds human beings together beneath the banner of a shared system of belief and practice. That binding occurs as the promise of immortality is realized: while Daniel and Isabelle's marriage dissolves when aging makes its first effects felt on Isabelle's body, rendering her undesirable and thus unlovable, for the "immortal" Elohimites the body of the other is never a source of disgust and separation, but always a source of desire and union. "Eternity, lovingly"—so goes the slogan of the Elohimite Church's advertising campaign (283). Love is only eternal, however, so long as the body is eternal: love is bound exclusively to the body, has its source in the body, and it is only by immortalizing the body that love can hope to endure.

Elohimism also fulfills the theological sense of religare, albeit in a limited or at the very least unconventional manner. In the place of a supernatural deity, Elohimism proposes the Elohim, a race of technologically superior extraterrestrials who the Elohimites believe created life on earth. Daniel1, who encounters the cult when he meets two practitioners during a dinner party in Spain, offers the following description:

> The couple were Elohimites, that is to say they belonged to a sect that worshipped the Elohim, extraterrestrial creatures responsible for the creation of mankind, and they were waiting for their return

> [. . .]. Essentially, according to them, everything boiled down to an error of transcription in the Book of Genesis: the creator, Elohi, was not to be taken in the singular, but in the plural. There was nothing divine or supernatural about our creators; they were simply material beings, more evolved than us, who had learned how to master space travel and the creation of life; they had also defeated aging and death [. . .]. (76–77)

The Elohimites of Daniel1's time do not live to see the return of their creators, and the neohumans of the fifth millennium still await the coming of these Future Ones. Different from their human predecessors, the neohumans practice a cult of emotional and sensual asceticism, attempting to eradicate whatever remnants of desire remain from their ancestors. This asceticism must be maintained until the arrival of the Future Ones, who alone can "succeed in joining the realm of countless potentialities" (334). Daniel24, struggling to suppress bouts of sentiment as he nears death, writes in his commentary on Daniel1's life story,

> The disappearance of social life was the way forward, teaches the Supreme Sister. It is no less the case that the disappearance of all physical contact between neohumans has been able to have [. . .] the character of an asceticism; moreover, this is precisely the term that the Supreme Sister uses in her messages [. . .]. Considering death, we have reached a state of mind that was, according to the monks of Ceylon, the one sought by the Buddhists of the Lesser Vehicle; our life at the moment of its end "is like blowing out a candle." We can also say, to use the words of the Supreme Sister, that our generations follow one another "like flicking the pages of a book." [. . .] I know that my asceticism will not have been in vain; I know that I will be part of the essence of the Future Ones. (115–16)

The restoration of human relationships, which the progressive isolation of the neohumans has made impossible, can only take place under the tutelage of the Future Ones. So long as the thoughts of the neohumans stay focused on the return of their creators, hope is sustained, and the ascetic rigor of their solitary existences remains bearable. Though disconnected from their peers, the neohumans of the fifth millennium are bound, in thought and contemplation, to the beings who created them—beings on whom their union, and thus felicity, depends entirely. The Elohim are not only humanity's creators and caretakers (as is the case for parents) but also its saviors. Faith in the existence of the Elohim and in the salvific benefits of their return to earth places the Elohimites in a binding relationship of hope and anticipation with these outworldly (though not otherworldly) beings. On the notion of religare alone, the religiosity of Elohimism cannot be denied.

The sacred and the profane. Émile Durkheim's understanding of religion rests on a distinction between the sacred and the profane. All religions, in Durkheim's view, maintain this dichotomy; consequently, all systems of belief and practice that posit sacred and profane entities are religions. Durkheim writes, "All known religious beliefs [. . .] have one characteristic in common: they imply a classification realized by man of things, real or ideal, into two classes—two contrasting genera usually designated by two distinct terms, which are well expressed by the words *profane* and *sacred*" (1994, 113). What typifies the relationship between the sacred and the profane is the radical heterogeneity between the two realms—for example, the difference between a wafer of bread and the holy host after a Catholic priest has consecrated it. Sacred things are of such a different order than profane things that the relationship between them may become one of antagonism. Durkheim adds, "The mind shrinks automatically from allowing the corresponding things to intermingle [. . .]. Such promiscuity or even close contiguity is strongly inconsistent with the state of dissociation surrounding these ideas in people's *consciousness*. The sacred thing is pre-eminently that which the profane must not and cannot touch with impunity" (1994, 116–17).

The Elohimite Church boasts no sacred chalices, holy relics, or pantheon of deities, but it does hold one object as being of higher value than all the rest: its adherents' DNA. The Elohimites take great care to ensure that each member's genetic code is preserved indefinitely. Replicated in five samples, the DNA is "preserved at low temperature in underground rooms impermeable to most known radiations, which could withstand a thermonuclear attack" (282). Similar to Christ buried in his tomb, the genetic material preserved in this underground laboratory awaits the day of its resurrection, when it will deliver to its owners the youthful, glorified bodies that the church has promised. DNA is the physical site of the sacred in the Elohimite religion. Its isolation in a subterranean laboratory only indicates the degree of that sanctity: hidden away and safe from human tampering, it belongs to a heterogeneous world of forbidden things, accessible only to the high priests of the faith (scientists, in the case of Elohimism), whose expertise permits them to handle this sacred material without risk of profaning it.

Elohimism also prescribes several rituals, the most consequential of which is the suicide rite that marks members' "entry into anticipation of resurrection" (249). Daniel25 writes in his commentary, "After a period of hesitation and uncertainty, the custom was gradually established of carrying it out in public, according to a simple, harmonious ritual, at a moment chosen by the follower, when he felt that his physical body was no longer in a state to give him the joys he could legitimately expect from it" (249). Besides evoking a parallel with early Christianity, in which hope for the resurrection of the body was matched by an equal certitude that Christ's return was imminent, the Elohimite suicide ritual sanctifies a death that might otherwise be experienced as arbitrary and meaningless. By choosing to end their lives on their own terms, adherents avoid suffering the slow degradation of aging and are able to escape an unpleasant embodiment in the company of their fellow believers, who affirm the soon-to-be departed in his or her hope for rebirth.

When one considers these practices in conjunction with the doctrine of the Elohim, the creators of all life; the existence of a prophet, who announces the return of the Elohim and their gift of immortality; and a host of minor rituals, practices, and beliefs, it is clear that Elohimism maintains the same distinction between the sacred and the profane that Durkheim theorized was characteristic of all religions. From this point of view, Elohimism is as much a religion as any other faith tradition: binding man to man as much as it binds man to a higher power, and prescribing practices and beliefs that sanctify the body in life, death, and resurrection, the church has all the sociological makings of a religion. And yet it is missing something, something too obvious to go unnoticed, even by the most Durkheimian of sociologists:

The supernatural. On first glance, Elohimism appears to distance itself radically from the supernatural: its "gods," the Elohim, are no more than highly evolved material beings, while the "souls" of its adherents are equated with memories contained in the physical brain. For the Elohimites, no forces exist that may "suspend, alter, or ignore" (Stark 2004, 10) the laws of nature; rather, it is precisely through the exploitation of those laws that immortality can be achieved. Miskiewicz, the church's leading scientist, describes Elohimite immortality thus:

> I suppose you [Daniel] remember what I said [. . .] concerning the neuro-circuits. Well, the reproduction of such a mechanism is

> possible, not in computers as we know them, but in a certain type of Turing machine, which we can call fuzzy automata [. . .]. Unlike classical calculators, fuzzy automata are capable of establishing variable, evolving connections between adjacent calculating units; they are therefore capable of memorization and apprenticeship. There is no a priori limit to the number of calculating units that can be linked, and therefore to the complexity of possible circuits. The difficulty at this stage [. . .] consists of establishing a bijective relation between the neurons of a human brain, taken in the few minutes following its death, and the memory of a nonprogrammed automaton. The life span of the latter being almost limitless, the next step will be to reinject the information in the opposite direction, toward the brain of the new clone; this is the *downloading* phase which [. . .] will present no particular difficulty once the *uploading* has been perfected. (92)

Miskiewicz's optimistic (not to mention rather burlesque) apology for machine-mind transfer might well be an example of scientistic fancy run amok. Such theories interest transhumanists who dream of uploading their brains into supercomputers, but the relationship of such thinking to real science is somewhat dubious.[5]

On supernatural criteria, Elohimism does not look like a religion at all. It may pass the Durkheimian test for religiosity, but the absence of any belief in the otherworldly distinguishes it not only from the monotheisms, where belief in the one God and the soul is central, but also from Buddhism and Hinduism, where some form of human identity survives bodily death to be reincarnated in the next life. If Elohimism is to be considered a religion according to the argument from the supernatural, some redefinition of the word "supernatural" will be needed. Such a reformulation is not, however, as unworkable as it may seem, for despite Elohimism's unswerving physicalist assumptions, it may still be possible to ascribe a sort of metaphorical supernaturalness to the movement. What Elohimism shares with the supernatural religions is the doctrine of survival—the continuing of existence, in some form, beyond the death of the body. The means of that survival are radically different: in the case of the supernatural religions, survival is a matter of fact, while for the Elohimites it must be artificially induced. But the object remains the same. Life beyond death is still possible; only the means of securing it have changed. Processes taken to be supernatural have, in effect, been naturalized, without altering the essence of the result. Simply put, in Elohimism it is precisely the *supernatural nature of the supernatural* that is called into question. By broadening the scope of the definition of "supernatural," we are thus able to grant Elohimism some provisional status as a religion.

A new synthesis. At least until recently, a common assumption in modern Western definitions of religion has been that religiosity is located within a discrete, identifiable sphere of cultural activity that the practitioner enters into knowingly in certain contexts (marriage, baptism, funeral, etc.), while at other times he or she exits that sphere and engages in other domains of cultural practice (the economic, political, familial, etc.). Clifford Geertz famously promulgates this understanding of religion in his 1973 book, *The Interpretation of Cultures*, in which he writes,

> To speak of the "religious perspective" is [. . .] to speak of one perspective among others. A perspective is a mode of seeing, in that extended sense of "see" in which it means "discern," "apprehend," "understand," or "grasp." It is a particular way of looking at life, a particular manner of construing the world, as when we speak of an historical perspective, a scientific perspective, an aesthetic perspective, a common-sense perspective [. . .]. The question then comes down to, first, what is the "religious perspective" generally considered, as differentiated from other perspectives; and second, how do men come to adopt it. (110)

Since the 1980s, however, this compartmentalized notion of religiosity has come under fire from critics who see in Geertz's rendering evidence of Christian and specifically Protestant bias. In particular, Talal Asad has argued that the very conditions out of which the need for a definition of religion arose were contingent on specific historical developments in the West, emerging in a post-Reformation environment in which "the religious" came to be visibly separated from "the secular." Asad explains,

> Several times before the Reformation, the boundary between the religious and the secular was redrawn, but always the formal authority of the Church remained preeminent. In later centuries, with the triumphant rise of modern science, modern production, and the modern state, the churches would also be clear about the need to

> distinguish the religious from the secular, shifting, as they did so, the weight of religion more and more onto the moods and motivations of the individual believer. Discipline (intellectual and social) would, in this period, gradually abandon religious space, letting "belief," "conscience," and "sensibility" take its place. (1993, 39)

Accordingly, any definition of religion that places at its center a "believer," who enters into a "religious perspective" under the influence of certain symbols, is in fact only a Christian and specifically Protestant formulation, which became necessary as secular culture increasingly undermined the political and "disciplinary" power of the church. Such a definition of religion would make little sense in a culture without a clear separation of the religious and the secular, and of the church and the state (as one finds, for example, in much of the Muslim world); indeed, there would be nothing to define, insofar as religion would remain embedded in a larger body of cultural practices.

Particularly revealing in relation to Houellebecq's treatment of religion is Asad's claim that "even a committed Christian cannot be unconcerned at the existence of truthful symbols that appear to be largely powerless in modern society. He will rightly want to ask: What are the conditions in which religious symbols can actually produce religious dispositions? Or, as a non-believer would put it: How does (religious) power create (religious) truth[?]" (1993, 33). In Houellebecq's novels, the power of religious and specifically Christian symbols (cathedrals, statues and other religious art, etc.) to generate enduring religious dispositions in the modern person is almost entirely absent. A character's confrontation with a religious symbol produces at best only fleeting nostalgia for a (largely romanticized) era of medieval piety, which dissipates as soon as he or she descends the steps of the church and emerges into the secular bustle of a busy Parisian street. Houellebecq describes this experience to Lévy: "How I loved, deeply loved the magnificent ritual, perfected over the centuries, of the mass! 'Lord, I am not worthy to receive you, but only say the word and I shall be healed.' Oh yes, certain words entered me, I received them into my heart. And for five or ten minutes every Sunday, I believed in God; and then I walked out of the church and it all disappeared, quickly, in a few minutes of walking through the streets in Paris" (2011, 138). Similarly, when, in *Submission*, François visits Notre Dame de Rocamadour, a famous pilgrimage site in southwestern France, the "religious mood" the visit engenders is of the most ephemeral, even tragic sort:

> The next morning, after loading my car, I returned to the now-deserted chapel. The Virgin waited in the shadows, calm and imperishable. She possessed dominion, she possessed power, but little by little I felt I was losing contact, that she was drifting away, disappearing into the centuries, while I slumped in my pew [. . .]. At the end of fifteen minutes I got up, permanently abandoned by the Spirit, reduced to my run-down, perishable body, and I sadly descended the steps in the direction of the parking lot. (2015a, 170, my translation)

Houellebecq's novels suggest that once religion becomes definable *as religion*—that is, once its symbols no longer address themselves to society at large as representative of discipline and moral authority, but rather address only the individual as motivators of religious "moods and motivations"—it is already doomed. Religion must do more than provide a space for the individual to enter, à la Geertz, into the "religious perspective." This is simply not enough for modern people; the symbols therein are too weak, too uncoupled from ordinary existence to give serious motivation. Religion must set a disciplinary canopy over the head of humankind, must order its acts and its moral commitments, must furnish ultimate explanations capable of determining the remainder of social life; otherwise, religion loses itself in the morass of competing perspectives (scientific, commonsense, political, etc.). This is precisely what has happened in the West and what Houellebecq attempts to rebuild under the guise of Elohimism.

Elohimism, Islam, and the Question of Religious Discipline

The disciplinary aspect of Elohimism only becomes apparent in the life stories of Daniel24 and Daniel25, copies of the original Daniel who live in isolation on remote, heavily guarded compounds following the apocalyptic collapse of global civilization. The clones form a loose confederation united by a Supreme Sister located in the mythical Central City. Physical contact between neohumans is prohibited; instead, they are expected to pass their lives in study of their forebears' life stories, and contact with other neohumans is limited to electronic communication.

The clones insist on a radical heterogeneity between themselves and the "human savages" who roam in small bands across the countryside. Daniel24 confesses, "For them I feel no pity, nor any sense of common belonging; I simply consider them to be slightly more intelligent monkeys, and, for this reason, more dangerous. There are times when I unlock the fence to rescue a rabbit, or a stray dog; but never to bring help to a human" (18). Having made a study of the lives of the "originals" (e.g., Daniel1), the neohumans have established a cult of strict asceticism intended to distance them from the destructive passions of their forebears, as well as to prepare them for the coming of the Future Ones (the Elohim). In order to endure lives of isolation, the clones have modified their genome to "decrease [. . .] the suffering linked to absence of contact" (115); even such fundamental elements of human nature as sexuality strike them as "genuine stumbling blocks" (226), as if they were children confused by a first course in sex education. The Supreme Sister, in echo (and perhaps parody) of Schopenhauer, outlines the ascetic program that each clone is expected to follow: "Jealousy, desire, and the appetite for procreation share the same origin, which is the suffering of being. It is the suffering of being which makes us seek out the other, as a palliative; we must go beyond this stage to reach the state where the simple fact of being constitutes in itself a permanent occasion for joy [. . .]. We must, in a word, reach the freedom of indifference, the condition for the possibility of perfect serenity" (260). As it is practiced by the neohumans, Elohimism is disciplinary insofar as its reach over individual existence appears to be total. The dyad of Supreme Sister and Central City governs every dimension of existence, from the social to the merely corporeal (recall the clones' altered genome), while departure from one's compound is an apostasy that results in the termination of one's genetic line (334).

The term "disciplinary" is, however, somewhat deceiving, or at the very least fraught with problematic assumptions about the role of religion in civilization. Elohimism is certainly not disciplinary in the sense that it is oppressing or colonizing its adherents for the sake of some material gain or for power for its own sake. Rather, the Supreme Sister's rigorous discipline is intended to separate this new humanity, physically and psychically, from the utter barbarism of the outside world, both as Daniel24 and 25 find that world in the fifth millennium and, more important, in its incipient form as Daniel1 conveys it in his life story. Daniel25 describes the process of cultural decay and finally collapse that has spanned the period between Daniel1's lifetime and the beginning of the fifth millennium: "Research has shown the resurgence, over this troubled period [the third millennium], of beliefs and behaviors from the most ancient folkloric past of Western mankind, such as astrology, divining magic, and fidelity to hierarchies of a dynastic type [. . .]. A violent, savage future was what awaited men, many were aware of it even before the unleashing of the first troubles" (310). Over the centuries, this renewal of barbarism has resulted in the disappearance of language and thus the loss of any form of "mental, intellectual, or artistic activity" (314). Reduced to animals, the remaining tribes display behaviors one might imagine to be typical of primordial humanity: "The tribe was organized along a strict hierarchical system [. . .]. The chief was a male of about forty, with graying hair; he was assisted by two young males who had rather broad chests, by far the biggest and most robust individuals in the group; copulation with the females was reserved for them: when the females encountered one of the three dominant males, they crouched down on all fours and presented their vulva" (318). Here, it is also helpful to recall the previously cited passage in which Daniel25, while wandering the Spanish countryside, encounters a fight to the death between the two oldest members of a tribe. The weaker of the two men is killed by the other, after which the men and women who have been watching the duel begin eating the still-writhing body and drinking the blood that has spilled onto the ground. Daniel25 observes, without irony, "all of this seemed to conform to what I had been taught about mankind" (321).

What Daniel25 has in mind, of course, is the already morally decayed civilization of Daniel1's time, when the elderly were left to die alone in ill-equipped nursing homes, and, once Elohimism took global hold, men and women as young as fifty began committing suicide in the hope of reincarnation in a younger body. The barbarism Daniel25 observes in the fifth millennium was, in other words, already well established at the outset of the third millennium, with the utter bestiality witnessed in the "savages" presented as the logical result of the materialist worldview that has progressively replaced Christianity in the modern period. No doubt it is unpopular today to view religion as a "civilizing force" that lifts humanity out of barbarism; rather, the prevailing tendency is to attribute to it somewhat the opposite function. Nevertheless, in *Possibility* Houellebecq presents Elohimism as the only institution capable of maintaining a semblance of civilization amid absolute disorder; indeed, it plays the "same role as the monasteries during the Middle Ages," maintaining history, science, and, most essentially, language (310). Upon finishing *Possibility*, the reader will perhaps wonder if we in the West have become so civilized that we have forgotten the terrible brutishness into which truly uneducated and uncultured man can descend. Houellebecq indicates that religion plays a critical role—disciplinary, authoritarian, or whatever one wishes to call it—in sparing us the worst of ourselves; the suggestion is not entirely unconvincing.

The ascendancy of Elohimism may also be an expression of increasingly explicit anxieties among Europeans about the spread of Islam in Europe, or what burgeoning far-right European political parties, such as France's National Front, often refer to as the "Islamicization" of the West. The Pew Forum on Religion and Public Life, for instance, reported in 2011 that by 2030 Muslims will make up 8 percent of the European population, up from approximately 6 percent in 2010, while in France the projection for 2030 is 10.2 percent, with Muslims in 2010 accounting for about 7.5 percent of the population. In the wake of the *Charlie Hebdo* attacks in January 2015 and the rise of the Islamic State in the Middle East, one can reasonably expect fears among many Europeans of an Islamic demographic and political conquest to increase. Houellebecq (2015b) has moderated his tone on Islam, granting that jihadists are "bad Muslims" and that a literal reading of the Quran does not necessarily lead to holy war. Throughout most of his career, however, he has been guilty of what many in the West refer to as "Islamophobia"—that is, of making statements both publicly and in his fiction that paint Islam in a less than flattering light.[6] It is worth spending a few moments reviewing them.

Houellebecq's most offending comments about Islam have been the object of significant legal and media controversy in France. Houellebecq has intellectual reasons for claiming Islam is the "stupidest religion"; his references on this point are such luminaries as Spinoza and Lévi-Strauss (see Houellebecq and Lévy 2011, 193). Monotheism is, for Houellebecq, "the act of a moron" (2001, n.p., my translation), a product of the desert and its one-dimensionality, invented by "filthy Bedouin[s]" who had nothing better to do than "bugger their camels" (2002, 179). Consequently, because Islam promotes the most strenuous form of monotheism, linked as it is to an intransigent legalism, it is the most deplorable of the monotheisms. What is, however, perhaps most interesting in Houellebecq's observations about Islam are not the tirades that readers find in *Platform*, but rather the few moments in his texts and public comments where he explicitly contrasts Islam to the culture of the contemporary West. For instance, in his 2001 *Lire* interview, Houellebecq opines, "Islam is a dangerous religion, and has been since its appearance. Fortunately, it is doomed. On the one hand, because God does not exist [. . .]. On the other hand, Islam is undermined from the inside by capitalism [. . .]. Materialism is a lesser evil. Its values are contemptible, but still less destructive, less cruel than those of Islam" (n.p., my translation).

Houellebecq has fashioned this hope for the rapid collapse of Islam into a talking point for a number of the Muslim characters in his novels. Unable to condemn Islam on his own without risk of causing a legal stir, Houellebecq allows fictional Muslims to do it for him. In *Platform*, Michel, having returned to Thailand after his lover Valérie's death at the hands of Muslim terrorists, listens to the following rant by a Jordanian banker:

> The problem with Muslims [. . .] was that the paradise promised by the Prophet already existed here on earth. There were places on earth where young, available, lascivious women danced for the pleasure of men, where one could become drunk on nectar and listen to celestial music; there were about twenty of them within five hundred yards of our hotel [. . .]. All you had to do was pay a couple of dollars [. . .]. For him, there was no doubt, the Muslim way was doomed: capitalism would triumph [. . .]. They might try to pretend otherwise, but secretly, [young Arab men] wanted to be part of the American system. The violence of some of them was no more than a sign of impotent jealousy, and thankfully, more and more of them were turning their backs on Islam. (2002, 250–51)

Here we are in the domain of prognostication and thus, in some sense, of anxiety; the collapse of Islam is historically inevitable, and as more and more Muslims become acquainted with the Western way of life, they are bound to abandon their "fearful" native religion for the freedoms of modernity.

In *Possibility*, this evolution is explicitly envisioned, with Islam only holding sway in Europe in the interim between the disappearance of Christianity and the rise of Elohimism. Having become "stronger in the Western countries at practically the same rate as Elohimism," Islam is able to convert indigenous Europeans en masse owing "uniquely to machismo" (246). "There were more and more people," Houellebecq writes, "especially women, who dreamed of a return to a system where women were modest and submissive, and their virginity was preserved" (246). While Elohimism also attracts converts from "the last residues from the fall of Christianity" (246) and then sets its sights on Asia, Islam in Europe "managed to assume [. . .] the role that had been Catholicism's in its heyday," "an 'official' religion, organizer of the calendar and of mini-ceremonies marking out the passage of time, with dogmas that were sufficiently primitive to be grasped by the greatest number while preserving sufficient ambiguity to seduce the most agile minds" (247). Islam's hegemony in the West is, however, brief. As "underground Internet connections" disseminate images throughout Muslim countries of a "way of life based on mass consumption, sexual freedom, and leisure, the enthusiasm of their populations was as intense and eager as it had been, half a century earlier, in the Communist countries" (248). Palestinian women in particular, who show a "sudden refusal [. . .] to limit their existence to the repeated procreation of future jihadists," initiate a broader revolt of Muslim youth that spreads to "all the Arab countries [. . .] in the face of which they obviously could do nothing" (248). "It then became perfectly clear, in the eyes of the Western populations, that all the countries of Dar-el-Islam had only been kept in their primitive faith by ignorance and constraint; deprived of their bases in the rear, the Western Islamist movements collapsed at a stroke" (248). No doubt these are bold predictions, and Islam's precipitous collapse in *Possibility* must surely be a source of pleasure (and relief) for readers unnerved by the contemporary proliferation of global jihad. Certainly one cannot prove that Houellebecq's treatment of Islam's demise issues from his anxieties; even without Elohimism's fortuitous appearance as an alternative to a defunct Christianity, Islam is the obvious favorite to become the next "official" religion of Europe—namely, a disciplinary institution that organizes social life in its most intimate aspects (i.e., sexual practices and the organization of time). *Possibility* reveals an assumption about the West's religious future in which Islam, without opposition from a new religious movement such as Elohimism, is the inevitable victor in the rush to fill Europe's religious vacuum. This assumption becomes all the more prescient in *Submission*: in this novel there are no Elohimites to vie for the heart, mind, and soul of the West.

To be sure, the reigning presuppositions are that secular humanism will continue as the West's metaphysical regime and that, with increasing globalization, one can reasonably expect it to spread. It is, however, always worth asking whether such a conjecture is warranted, and Houellebecq's novels are uniquely suited to engage readers in a salubrious reappraisal of the fundamental values embedded in post-Christian Western liberal discourse. Increasing freedom always and everywhere signifies increasing happiness, the joys of liberation are not undermined by the anxieties it produces, humanity is happier without God than with him—these are the deeply secular, deeply liberal assumptions that Houellebecq's novels take to task. Transgressiveness as a literary trope is usually attributed to writers and texts that bend and distort the limits of freedom in the direction of even greater liberation.

In Houellebecq's case, transgressiveness moves in the opposite direction, scandalously daring us to wonder if the discourse of human dignity and rights that the West has fashioned in the wake of God's death can remain the guarantor of human happiness, or whether, as the Comtean understanding of history holds, it is no more than a wobbly metaphysical placeholder awaiting the shattering day of God's return.

Religion and Utopia

Deep down, I am with the utopians, people who think that the movement of *History* must conclude in an absence of movement. An end to *History* seems desirable to me.

—**Quoted in Varsava 2005**

Houellebecq's concern with the spiritual future of the West is foreign to much of mainstream twentieth-century intellectualism. At least in France, the middle decades of that century saw an intellectual milieu preoccupied with Marxism, Maoism, and the ideals of 1968 and devoted to some form of secular socialism. Sartre's claim at the end of *Existentialism Is a Humanism* that "[e]xistentialism is merely an attempt to draw all of the conclusions inferred by a consistently atheistic point of view" (2007, 53) would seem a proper summary of the period's intellectual commitments: God removed from the human scene and with him the possibility of founding any notion of rights or essence—with the additional consequence that humanity is now free to fashion itself according to its own will, without regard for Providence. Freedom from divine will is as old as modernity, but in the case of philosophers such as Sartre (and certainly the Marxists of the subsequent generation of intellectuals, among whom were Althusser, Bourdieu, and Foucault), freedom came with the added requirement of radical self-determination. Claims to essence were the product of dominant bourgeois institutions and the so-called sites of power they concealed. The task of the intellectual was to unmask and render intelligible those mechanisms of power in the interest of liberating the human being from bourgeois slave drivers. Such was basically the work of Foucault and, in a different era, Marx.

For historical reasons that I will not elucidate here, prominent segments of the French intelligentsia—specifically those in public view—eventually abandoned intellectual Marxism, first for Maoism, in light of revelations about Stalin, and then, following revelations about Mao, in favor of a new humanist movement led by such *nouveaux philosophes* as Bernard-Henri Lévy and André Glucksmann. Belief in history and the dialectic has since dropped off much of the French intellectual radar, but the problem of godlessness remains. As Lévy writes in his 2009 book, *Left in Dark Times*, lamenting the disarray of today's European left, "No other heaven, ever again. No more uncreated truths, of any kind [. . .]. We have to imagine happy atheists. [. . .] That's the price of democracy" (211). The fundamental dilemma persists: how to legitimate morality and the social order on the basis of rights that have no divine sanction. Marxists have history. Liberals have humanism. Believers have God. That is a hard act to follow.

The political concerns of Houellebecq's novels are famously difficult to distribute to traditional notions of right and left. Houellebecq's fiction, as Bruno Viard (2008, 38) has pointed out, seems simultaneously to appeal to both sides of the political spectrum, condemning simultaneously the excesses of consumer capitalism and those of the liberation of values, especially in the domain of sexuality. It must be kept in mind, however, that the intellectual and political evolution outlined above, from atheistic Marxism à la Sartre to atheistic humanism à la Lévy, does not serve as Houellebecq's ideological starting point. In Houellebecq's fiction, both movements represent unsuccessful attempts to sanction morality and justify the social order in the absence of God, basing their claims about what constitutes human happiness on an economic conception of human nature. Subsequently, both movements fail, one at the political level, the other at the moral level. Social collapse in the Houellebecquian universe occurs in the transition from a theological to an economic understanding of the human being, not in the alternations between socialism and liberalism, however calamitous these may be. A passage from *The Map and the Territory* describing the final hours of capitalism speaks to the insolvency of all economic conceptions of humankind: "You were living in an ideologically strange period, when everyone in Western Europe seemed persuaded that capitalism was doomed [. . .] without, however, the ultra-left parties managing to attract anyone beyond their usual clientele of spiteful masochists" (2012, 251).

In order to understand the point of departure of the Houellebecquian critique of the West, one must go back before Althusser, before Sartre and Camus, before even Marx, and return to the socialist utopians of the early nineteenth century (specifically Fourier and Saint-Simon), to the revolutionaries (Maximilien Robespierre in particular), and, of course, to Comte. Socialism from Marx onward turns to atheism; socialism before Marx was part of a larger effort to fill the religious vacuum that had been left by the revolution. Houellebecq's fiction partakes in this effort, even though it does so in the dissimilar context of contemporary consumerist society.

The Fresh Ruins of France

Since Marx, it has been customary to equate socialism with atheism and to conceive of religion as contrary to progressive political agendas.[1] However, much of French utopian thought during the nineteenth century was religious in character, with only Marx and Engels representing a definitive move toward materialism. Charles Fourier, for example, includes a robust spiritual cosmology in his utopian prescriptions for overcoming the evils of capitalism and bourgeois domesticity. In the creation of the world, God established a complex system of "passionate attraction" that, once realized in the social order, would usher in an era of human harmony; indeed, the souls of the dead wait "expectantly for the triumph of [passionate] attraction on earth" so that they can "reappear on some more fortunate globe" (Manuel and Manuel 1979, 647).

Claude-Henri de Saint-Simon, the father of the Saint-Simonian movement, also recruits religion in his attempts to elaborate a utopian vision for a nineteenth century plagued by *mal de siècle* spiritual angst. Saint-Simon spent much of his career as a propagandist for bourgeois industrialism, and it was only in his late writings that a religious element began clearly to emerge. In "Nouveau Christianisme," his last published work, Saint-Simon calls for the establishment of a new form of Christianity cured of its errant theologizing and metaphysical pitfalls and directed solely at "the most rapid betterment of the welfare of the poorest class" (1997, 118, my translation). Auguste Comte, meanwhile, though a militant atheist, imagines a religion of humanity centered around worship of the social body and capable of reproducing Catholicism's social-structuring (i.e., disciplinary) power. Finally, Maximilien Robespierre's promulgation of the Cult of the Supreme Being bespoke fears among the revolutionaries that Jacobin atheism would poison the republican project. In his address to the convention on May 7, 1794, Robespierre declares, "Let us leave behind priests and return to divinity. Let us attach morality to sacred and eternal foundations; let us inspire in man that religious respect for man [. . .] which is the sole guarantee of social happiness" (1989, 324, my translation).[2]

Echoes exist throughout Houellebecq's fiction of the attempts by Fourier, Saint-Simon, Comte, and Robespierre to combine social progress with a religious ethos, and below I address each author's principal ideas in conjunction with the utopianism in Houellebecq's novels. Comte will figure last, since his *Religion of Humanity* represents a point of transition between the more theistic socialism of Fourier and Saint-Simon and the atheistic socialism of Marx.

Maximilien Robespierre. In addition to providing a model of political terrorism to which he himself was to fall victim—Robespierre was guillotined in July 1794 after losing the support of the convention—Robespierre also created a prototype for religious innovation in the form of the Cult of the Supreme Being, a deistic cult inspired in part by the philosophy of Jean-Jacques Rousseau.[3] Robespierre's aim in promulgating the cult was largely to combat radical de-Christianizing elements among the revolutionaries, who had imbibed the atheistic and materialistic vitriol of radical enlightenment figures, such as Spinoza, Diderot, and La Mettrie (Israel 2002, 717–18). In his address of May 7, 1794, Robespierre may well have had such figures in mind when he spoke before the convention. He declares,

> Who gave you as a mission to announce to the people that Divinity does not exist, O you who have a passion for this arid doctrine, but who never take an avid interest in the fatherland? What advantage do you find in persuading man that a blind force presides over his destiny, and strikes at random crime and virtue; that his soul is only a breath of air that is extinguished at the gates of death? [. . .] Miserable sophist! By what right do you come stripping from innocence the scepter of reason in order to place it back in the hands of crime, to throw a funereal shroud over nature, push sorrow to despair, delight vice, sadden virtue, degrade humanity? (1989, 316)

For Robespierre, atheism represents a "conspiracy against the Republic" (317), and thus it is of vital interest that "the French people recognize the existence of the Supreme Being, and the immortality of the soul" (329). The Cult of the Supreme Being was thus in many respects a precursor to attempts in the nineteenth century to offer "rational" alternatives to the "God of the priests" (Catholicism; 323), which Robespierre expressly condemns.

Like Robespierre, Houellebecq has conveyed unmistakable anxiety about the viability of a society from which religion has been removed. Cutting society off from its religious foundations is "tantamount to suicide" (2011, 161), Houellebecq claims to Lévy, while Djerzinski in *Particles* wonders how long Western civilization can endure after the collapse of Christianity (2000a, 135). In *The Possibility of an Island*, these anxieties give birth to the Elohimite Church, which is able to replace the world's decaying faith traditions during the course of the twenty-first century by promising physical and psychic immortality through cloning. The belief in immortality is central to the Elohimites' conception of religion, and more than anything it is humanity's insatiable desire for eternal life, rather than for moral order, that fuels the movement's success: "The idea of immortality had basically never been abandoned by man, and even though he may have been forced to renounce his old beliefs, he had still kept, close to him, a nostalgia for them, he had never given up, and he was ready, in return for any explanation, however unconvincing, to let himself be guided by a new faith" (2007, 249).

For both Houellebecq and Robespierre, the existential burdens of materialism and atheism are unbearable, and each man does his best to fashion an alternative to the threat of a religious vacuum. Robespierre's Cult of the Supreme Being associates a belief in immortality with the possibility of moral order, the one being necessary for the other, whereas in *Possibility* the pursuit of eternal life takes a resolutely more hedonistic tone. The comparison is, of course, somewhat limited, for Robespierre both believed in his solution to materialism and atheism and possessed, if only briefly, the political means to realize it, while Houellebecq's fictional experiment in human cloning in *Possibility* ends with Daniel25's decision to abandon the neohuman cult. Nonetheless, the comparison does show that concern over the nefarious social consequences of disbelief has deep roots in France's political and intellectual past and that Houellebecq's particular rendering of them, though removed from a revolutionary context, shares a certain lineage with forms of revolutionary thought that have identified materialism as a roadblock to social order.

Charles Fourier. In *Houellebecq au laser: La faute à Mai 68*, Bruno Viard describes Houellebecq's rapprochement between sexual and economic competition in *Whatever* as "totally unusual" (2008, 41, my translation). In the novel's account, just as economic competition creates a hierarchy between those who possess monetary wealth and those who do not, so sexual competition introduces disparities between those with great sexual capital (the young, the beautiful, the virile) and those with little (the ugly, the disabled, the old). In societies where adultery is permitted, phenomena of "absolute pauperization" (Houellebecq 2011, 99) in matters of sex will therefore appear. Those with a large amount of sexual capital will have access to sex nearly every day, while those without such capital will be placed in a situation of forced abstinence:

> Economic liberalism is an extension of the domain of the struggle, its extension to all ages and all classes of society. Sexual liberalism is likewise an extension of the domain of the struggle, its extension to all ages and all classes of society [. . .]. Certain people win on both levels; others lose on both. Businesses fight over certain young professionals; women fight over certain young men; men fight over certain young women; the trouble and strife are considerable. (99)

Twentieth-century capitalism is to blame for these developments, for during this period individualism and liberal morality combined with the powerful desire-engineering tools of modern advertising to create the "social superstore" (Houellebecq 2009, 27–28, my translation). In times past, the parameters of sexual exchange were "dependent on a lyrical, impressionistic, and not very reliable system of description," whereas today sexual commerce has been reduced to "simple and objectively verifiable criteria" (30, my translation). Choosing a sexual partner has become similar to choosing a piece of meat at the supermarket. Those with the greatest amount of sexual capital quickly devour the freshest, most succulent portions, while the insipid, expired meat is shrink-wrapped and consigned to some gloomy refrigerator that no one will ever open, finally to be tossed into the oven and incinerated once its market value is completely gone.

Whatever's depiction of a sexuality ruled by market forces is not so unusual as we might think, so long as one takes "unusual" to mean "unique." Charles Fourier, perhaps the most creative of all nineteenth-century social reformers, prefigures much of Houellebecq's discourse on sexuality in his prescriptions for sexual utopia in the community of the phalanx.[4] Jonathan Beecher writes, "In Harmony [. . .] every mature man and woman must be guaranteed a satisfying minimum of sexual pleasure. Whatever his or her age and no matter how bizarre his or her desires, no Harmonian could go unsatisfied" (1990, 305). Given his time and place, Fourier does not offer a strict parallel between sexuality and the market economy, but many of his comments indicate an implicit rapprochement of the two terms. Fourier writes, "Reason [. . .] has done nothing for man's happiness so long as it has not given social man that fortune which is the subject of all longing: and by SOCIAL FORTUNE I mean a graded opulence that spares the least wealthy men hardship and which guarantees them at least as a *minimum* the fate which we call BOURGEOIS MEDIOCRITY" (1953, 134, my translation).[5] In Fourier's view, reasonable access to sex is considered a part of bourgeois mediocrity.

Reason, and by extension modernity, whose technological prowess and economic might are unmatched in any other period of human history, have given us progress but not a basic equality of means, either material or sexual. Tisserand of *Whatever*, for example, has access to all the amenities and material comforts of modern existence—he even has the means to pay for prostitutes—but his ugliness forbids him the slightest possibility of finding love (or, at the very least, someone who *desires* to have sex with him, which in Houellebecq's novels often counts for as much). Tisserand admits to the narrator, "I've done my sums, you see; I've got enough to pay for one whore a week; Saturday evening, that'd be good. Maybe I'll end up doing it. But I know that some men can get the same thing for free, *and with love to boot*. I prefer trying; for the moment I still prefer trying" (98).

Sensitive to the sexual injustices visited upon those like Tisserand who possess meager erotic capital, Fourier makes provision for a "cadre of civil servants of the two sexes" in the phalanx, "a quasi-religious and particularly respected order [. . .] who would satisfy charitably, if not at an hourly rate, the amorous needs of the old, of the abandoned, of those whom nature had disgraced" (Armand 1953, 29, my translation). As a part of the new sexual order envisioned for the phalanx, Fourier calls for the creation of a court of love whose members would see to the erotic satisfaction of all members of the community (Beecher 1990, 309). Provision is even made for the elderly. While in *Possibility*, the age difference represents "the last taboo," and it is "forbidden to be *old*" (148), Fourier declares, "In Harmony [. . .] no one is poor and all may be admitted to love's favors until a very advanced age" (1967, 263).

The practice of erotic philanthropy also finds echo in *Platform*, where Houellebecq portrays Asian prostitutes as a professional erotic elite who service sexually frustrated Westerners no longer able to find physical satisfaction in their home countries. The narrator, Michel, opines to Jean-Yves,

> [Y]ou have several hundred million westerners who have everything they could want but no longer manage to obtain sexual satisfaction. They spend their lives looking without finding it, and they are completely miserable. On the other hand, you have several billion people who have nothing, who are starving, who die young, who live in conditions unfit for human habitation, and who have nothing left to sell except their bodies and their unspoiled sexuality. It's simple, really simple to understand: it's an ideal trading opportunity. (2002, 173)

Different from Fourier's conception of the relationship between the sexual philanthropist and his or her client, in *Platform* it is market forces rather than compassionate giving that govern the exchange between client and prostitute. In *Platform*'s version of sexual utopia, the relationship between the two parties is based on the parameters of economic exchange—imposed by the practice of sex tourism—whereas for Fourier it is rooted in the notion of charity. Even so, Houellebecq does at times evoke charity as a principal sexual motivation. For example, when Bruno in *Particles* tells Christiane the story of his attempt to seduce a teenage student in his class, Christiane says, "we need a little generosity. Someone has to start. If I'd been in the Arab girl's place, I don't know how I would have reacted. But I believe there was something genuine about you even then. [. . .] well, I hope I would've consented to give you pleasure" (2000a, 166). In Houellebecq's depictions of sex, it is often a lack of erotic charity that leads Westerners to the extremes the reader encounters in *Platform*. The Eldorador Aphrodite resort stands as a kind of substitute for the court of love that Fourier imagines, for any inkling of charity on the part of the prostitute is subsumed under the greater need for monetary gain.

Houellebecq's affinities with Fourier go beyond the two authors' treatments of sexual inequality. Women for both Houellebecq and Fourier are not the fairer sex but quite simply the *better* sex, and social progress depends not on the mere participation of women in the social order but on their ascendancy. Fourier, who coined the term "feminism," claims that "the extension of women's privileges is the general principle of all social progress" and insists that women, once placed "in a state of freedom," will surpass men "in all the functions of mind and body that are not the attributes of physical strength" (1953, 124–25). Houellebecq's novels evoke Fourier's analysis, though there the celebration of female nature is often as focused on maternity as it is on intelligence. During one of his more catatonic moments, Djerzinski reflects in *Particles*,

> Amid the vile filth, the ceaseless carnage which was the lot of animals, the only glimmer of devotion and altruism was the protective maternal instinct [. . .]. The female squid, a pathetic little thing barely twenty centimeters long, unhesitatingly attacks the diver who comes near her eggs. [. . .] [W]omen were indisputably better than men. They were gentler, more affectionate, loving and compassionate; they were less prone to violence, selfishness, cruelty or self-centeredness. Moreover, they were more rational, intelligent and hardworking. (137)

In Djerzinski's perspective, modern man is reduced to a sperm donor, a creature whose only biological utility, beyond reproducing the species, lies in his now-obsolete ability to defend women and children from bears:

> What on earth were men for, Michel wondered [. . .]. In earlier times, when bears were more common, perhaps masculinity had served a particular and irreplaceable function, but for centuries now men clearly served no useful purpose. For the most part they assuaged their boredom playing tennis, which was a lesser evil; but from time to time they felt the need to *change history*—which basically meant inciting revolutions and wars [. . .]. A world of women would be immeasurably superior, tracing a slower but unwavering progress, with no U-turns and no chaotic insecurity, toward a general happiness. (137)

Houellebecq is in total agreement with his protagonist here. Alongside the good news that he announces in *The Elementary Particles* is the declaration that "women continue to be strangely capable of love, and it seems to me desirable that we should return to a matriarchal society. Men are good for nothing, with the exception, at present, of being able to reproduce the species" (Houellebecq 1998, n.p., my translation).

This view is a radicalization of Fourier's, for the latter never advocated a matriarchal society, nor did he consider men to be useless biological anachronisms. But both authors agree that the prevalence of female nature over male nature is a prime indicator of social progress. Moreover, feminism of the sort Simone de Beauvoir advocated only pushes women to imitate the worst in men: careerism, infidelity, egotism, and so on. In "L'Humanité, second stade," his 1998 introduction to a French translation of Valerie Solanas's radical feminist pamphlet, the *SCUM Manifesto* (1968), Houellebecq writes,

> For my part I've always considered feminists to be lovable idiots, inoffensive in principle but unfortunately made dangerous by their disarming absence of lucidity. As such one could see them struggling in the 1970s for contraception, abortion, sexual freedom, etc., all as if the "patriarchal system" was the invention of evil males, while the historical objective of men was obviously to fuck the maximum number of chicks without having to take on the burden of a family. The poor dears pushed their naïveté even to the point of imagining that lesbian love, an erotic condiment appreciated by the near-totality of active heterosexuals, was a dangerous questioning of masculine power. Finally they demonstrated [. . .] an incomprehensible appetite for the professional world and company life; men, who for a long time knew what to make of the "freedom" and "blossoming" offered by work, snickered gently. (2009, 165, my translation)

On this account, women-to-work feminism only casts women headlong into the jowls of the market, where their female nature is trampled and finally destroyed. If society is to move beyond the barbarity of capitalism, women must not simply be equal to men, materially and economically speaking, but rather must surpass them in virtue and intelligence by exploiting their own particularly feminine nature.

Other commonalities between Fourier and Houellebecq include the writers' treatments of childhood and parenting, human rights, and the numerical particulars of social organization. In Fourier's phalanx, children were to be separated from adults and made to eat and sleep in different rooms; "parents will take all the more pleasure in doting over them in that they will see them less" (Armand 1953, 29, my translation). In *The Possibility of an Island*, Fourier's recommendation is radicalized in the form of "child-free zones," which Houellebecq describes as residences created for "guiltless thirtysomethings who confessed frankly that they could no longer stand the screams, dribbles, excrement, and other environmental inconveniences that usually accompanied *little brats*" (46). In Fourier's account, child-rearing is a needless imposition on adults' happiness and should be entrusted to the care of willing professionals; parents will love their children more for having to see them less, while in *Possibility* the reader has the impression that certain parents do not love their children at all!

Fourier and Houellebecq also demonstrate similar incredulity toward the notion of rights. For Fourier (1996, 280), "equality is the cause that mows down three million young men," and morality is the "fifth wheel on a cart," the concept of which only exists because human beings have hitherto been unable to establish a natural harmony among themselves (Jones and Patterson 1996, xix–xx). Similarly, in *The Elementary Particles* and *The Possibility of an Island*, both neohuman communities disparage the notion of human rights, with social harmony in *Particles* being achieved not through an evolution in mentalities or a renewed commitment to "human dignity," but rather by breeding out those characteristics of the human species, primarily selfishness and individualism, that had necessitated the creation of the myth of natural rights during the materialist age. For Fourier, modification of social organization is the key to harmony. In Houellebecq's fiction, such harmony depends on modification of the human genome—a shift in technological possibility rather than in philosophy. In both cases, the institution of rights is necessary only where natural harmony cannot be achieved.

Finally, we find in Fourier and Houellebecq's utopian scenarios a curious preoccupation with numbers. Fourier identifies 810 personality types and insists that each phalanx be composed of approximately 1,600 members, the ideal number being 1,620 (1953, 136). In *Particles* Djerzinski proposes that the number of neohumans always be a prime number, divisible only by itself and one—a symbolic warning against subgroups: "the number of individuals in the new species must always be a prime number; it is therefore necessary to create one person, then two, then three, then five [. . .]. The purpose of having a population divisible only by itself and one was meant to draw symbolic attention to the dangers which subgroups constitute in any society" (261). Houellebecq and Fourier only differ significantly on the question of Providence. God is absent from the utopias of *Particles* and *Possibility*, whereas he has a role to play in Harmony. If Houellebecq has more openly aligned himself with the atheistic positivism of Auguste Comte, it is no doubt due to this fundamental difference.

Claude-Henri de Saint-Simon. Like Charles Fourier, Saint-Simon envisions his utopia in religious terms. In Saint-Simon's case, however, bringing about earthly paradise depends not on the arcane metaphysical abstractions of Fourier's theories of harmony and passionate attraction, but rather on a concerted "detheologizing" of the Christian faith. The connection between Houellebecq and Saint-Simon is more analogical than literal, for never in Houellebecq's novels does one discover any interest in rejuvenating Christianity, and, like Comte, Houellebecq does not hold out a hope of eternal life. Rather, the comparison to be drawn between the two writers relates to their broader attitudes toward metaphysics and individualism, both symptoms of the collapse of medieval civilization and the ensuing epistemological confusion of modernity.

Central to Saint-Simon's criticism of contemporary Christianity was his assertion that both its Catholic and Protestant versions were heresies. Catholicism had allowed itself to become obsessed with theological and doctrinal minutiae (Saint-Simon 1997, 126), while Protestantism had diminished the social importance of Christianity by placing the personal relationship between human and God above the good of society (158). Gaining eternal life is no more a matter of reciting prayers in Latin, eating fish on Fridays, or self-flagellation than it is of professing the proper creed (153–54). Instead, admittance to God's eternal kingdom hinges on one's commitment to bettering the human species, especially its poorest classes: "True Christianity commands all men to behave as brothers to each other; Jesus Christ has promised eternal life to those who shall have most contributed to the amelioration of the existence of the poorest class on the moral and physical level" (115, my translation).[6] Saint-Simon's gospel, which he calls "Nouveau Christianisme," is more social than theological: once the "purification" of Christianity is complete—that is, once the religion has been freed from its theological fetters and social morality has become the principal duty and concern of the believer—Christianity could be employed to combat political powers that privilege personal and private interests at the expense of the general good (163). The Catholic Church had promoted dogma over social justice and was concerned with a heavenly paradise at the expense of the kingdom of God on earth (163). Reformed Christianity, on the other hand, had placed one's relationship with God above one's duty to society, putting Christianity "outside the bounds of social organization" (158). Both traditions depart from the humanistic, worldly message of the Gospels, and thus Saint-Simon considers them heretical.

For Houellebecq, the dangers of metaphysics lie not in ecclesiastical obscurantism but rather in the ontology of materialism pervading modernity. Saint-Simon preaches that the only sure path to salvation is service to humanity's most downtrodden classes; accordingly, he presents his doctrine as "called upon [. . .] to anathematize theology, to classify as impious any doctrine whose object it is to teach men means of gaining eternal life other than that of working with all their strength for the betterment of their fellow man's existence" (1997, 154). In *The Elementary Particles*, the entry into eternal life—that is, into the life of the new clone society—requires a repudiation of the "metaphysics of materialism" in favor of a new understanding of reality in which the notions of matter and separation are replaced by new concepts of interweaving and infinite belonging. Djerzinski writes in his fictitious *Meditations on Interweaving*,

> Uneducated man [. . .] is terrified of the idea of space; he imagines it to be vast, dark and yawning. He imagines beings in the elementary forms of spheres, isolated in space, curled up in space, crushed by the eternal presence of three dimensions [. . .]. In this space of which they are so afraid, human beings learn how to live and die; in their mental space, separation, distance and suffering are born [. . .]. Love binds, and it binds forever. Good binds, while evil unravels. Separation is another word for evil; it is also another word for deceit. All that exists is a magnificent interweaving, vast and reciprocal. (251)

By repudiating supposedly metaphysical notions, such as matter, dimensionality, and space, the human being realizes his or her absolute interconnectivity with the rest of the human world. The metaphysics of materialism, inherited from Newtonian conceptions of matter but superseded by the revelations of quantum physics, do no more than stand in the way of an honest appraisal of human ontology and the means of improving it. For Saint-Simon, the metaphysics of church dogma distract the believer's attention from social justice and draw it toward his or her reward in the world to come. In *Particles*, the belief in matter must be abandoned if humanity is to overcome the forces of social atomization and be born anew in an era of infinite intersubjectivity.

Both Houellebecq and Saint-Simon trace the rise of modern individualism to the decline of Christianity at the end of the medieval period. Saint-Simon argues that the transition from the Middle Ages to modernity represented a gradual relinquishment of social concerns in favor of individual rights:

> From the establishment of Christianity until the fifteenth century, the human species concerned itself principally with the harmonization of its general sentiments [. . .]. Since the fifteenth century, the human mind has broken loose of the most general views; it has given itself over to specialties, it has concerned itself with the analysis of the personal matters, the private interests of the different classes of society [. . .] and, during this second period, the opinion has been established that considerations about general facts, about the general principles and general interests of the human species, were only vague and metaphysical considerations, unable to contribute to the progress of enlightenment [. . .]. (1997, 184)

Houellebecq renders the phenomenon somewhat more obliquely, though like Saint-Simon he marks the beginning of the decline in the fifteenth century:

> Though it may be difficult for us to understand this now, it is important to remember how central the notions of "personal freedom," "human dignity" and "progress" were to people in the age of materialism (defined as the centuries between the decline of medieval Christianity and the publication of Djerzinski's work). The confused and arbitrary nature of these ideas meant, of course, that they had little practical or social function—which might explain why human history from the fifteenth to the twentieth centuries was characterized by progressive decline and disintegration. (2000a, 258–59)

The transition to our era of individual concerns is thus a process of moral and social deterioration. As it has moved away from medieval Christianity, Western civilization has become progressively atomized, attempting to grant attention to the limited concerns of individual parties. Human rights are an ad hoc replacement for divine sanction, and their failure to have any "practical or social function" lies in the problem of their legitimation. The difference between Houellebecq and Saint-Simon is merely in their choice of terms: where Saint-Simon speaks of secondary principles, Houellebecq invokes the concept of rights. Both are unsatisfactory alternatives to a divine power capable of commanding the social order.

Fourier's and Saint-Simon's prescriptions for social progress and reorganization are accompanied by theological elements that, though not always formulated in explicit creedal statements, make both thinkers' utopianism religious and dualistic in character. For Fourier, human relationships are to be harmonized according to the laws of passionate attraction, which God set forth in his design of the universe. In Saint-Simon's case, the improvement of the condition of the poor requires maintaining allegiance to the original intent of the Gospels and focusing Christianity on social justice rather than on theological abstractions. Fourier and Saint-Simon also hold out hope for nonabstract forms of eternal life, which distinguishes them significantly from the utopian and social theory of Comte. In Fourier's case, the earth's departed hover about their home planet in the hope that their incarnate brethren will achieve harmony; for Saint-Simon, and especially for the explicitly religious Saint-Simonian movement that followed his death, the rewards of the world to come are linked to one's treatment of this world's poor. Houellebecq may follow these thinkers in their worries over capitalism and metaphysics, their celebration of the feminine, and their critique of individualism, but he cannot embellish his representations of utopia with allusions to the will of a creator God or with a promise of eternal life beyond the physical body. It is only in Comte, whose thought shares so much with his utopian predecessors yet whose atheism and physicalism represent an evolution toward the secular socialism of Marxism, that Houellebecq finds a true ally.

Auguste Comte. Widely credited with having invented the field of sociology, Comte is today known principally as the originator of the *loi des trois étapes*, or law of the three stages. Comte's vast philosophy, presented in his massive *Course in Positive Philosophy* (1830–42) and the more succinct *General View of Positivism* (1848), holds that civilization has progressed through three stages of historical development: the theological, the metaphysical, and finally the scientific or "positive." The theological stage was the pre-Enlightenment and prerevolutionary period of European history, when the will of God (refracted, to be sure, through the policies of the church) was the final word in matters of justice and morality.

In the subsequent metaphysical stage, which Comte associates with postrevolutionary France, the notion of "rights" began to emerge as a replacement for divine sanction. Comte considers the doctrine of human rights set forth during the revolution to represent a groping for a new principle in which to root notions of morality and social order; rights are necessarily vague and abstract in character, having no divine sanction from which to derive their authority, but they nonetheless reveal an effort on the part of postrevolutionary society to escape the arbitrariness of divine will. Thus, in Comte's perspective, the striving for clarity and emancipation inherent in the metaphysical stage leads to a positive era in which the notion of rights disappears in favor of a system of morality based on a "science of society."

The positive stage culminates in the religion of humanity, a secular-religious system centered on the worship of the social body and intended, much like Robespierre's Cult of the Supreme Being, to offer an alternative to what Comte perceives to be a defunct Catholicism. Comte embellishes his religion with a positivist calendar and creates a "positivist catechism" that mimics Catholicism in its inclusion of seven sacraments and a "holy trinity," replacing Father, Son, and Holy Spirit with Altruism, Order, and Progress. Comte's new religion met with some success in France and Brazil, but like other secular alternatives to religion that emerged during the nineteenth century, its social significance today is all but nonexistent.

Comte views monotheism as nothing less than social poison. Not only does it represent the vestiges of "initial theologism" (the primitive worldview of both the prepositive and premetaphysical eras; 1968, 330), but monotheism's continuing influence also directly impedes progress. Comte is unsparing in his condemnation:

> Their God has become the [. . .] leader of a hypocritical conspiracy, now more ridiculous than odious, which is trying hard to distract the people from all great social improvements by preaching to them a fanciful compensation [. . .]. Every theological trend, Catholic, Protestant, or deist, leads in reality to the prolongation and aggravation of moral anarchy, while impeding the decisive influence of social sentiment and collective spirit [. . .]. There is now no subversive utopia that does not take root or sanction in monotheism. (398)

The monotheistic camp is, for Comte, "retrograde and anarchic," a domain where "God presides vaguely," while the religion of humanity, freed from all theological fetters and from vain talk of "fanciful compensation" (i.e., personal immortality), is "organic and progressive, systematically devoted to Humanity" (398).

From his declaration in *Lire* that monotheism is the "act of a moron" to the Egyptian biochemist's rant against Islam in *Platform*, Houellebecq has demonstrated in both fiction and nonfiction a loyalty to atheism that only finds nuance in his most recent public comments (see chapter 5). For example, in "J'ai un rêve," a short essay describing his personal version of eternal life, Houellebecq writes,

> In my dream of eternal life, nothing much happens. Perhaps I'm living in a cave. Yes, I like caves, inside they're dark and cool and I feel safe. I often wonder if there has been any real progress since the time of cavemen. As I'm seated there, listening calmly to the sound of the sea, surrounded by friendly creatures, I think of all the things I'd like to remove from this world: fleas, birds of prey, money and work. Also probably porno films and belief in God. (2009, 179–80, my translation)

But however much Houellebecq may denigrate the notion of the one God in certain comments, he nevertheless laments God's absence in other places.

Particularly liable to disparagement is Comte's abstract vision of eternal life, wherein personal immortality is replaced by a theoretical perpetuation in human memory—what Comte refers to as the sacrament of "Incorporation":

> Comte [. . .] failed totally and miserably. A religion with no God may be possible [. . .]. But none of this seems to me to be conceivable without a belief in eternal life, the belief that in all monotheistic religions acts as the great *introductory offer*, because once you've conceded that, and with this as your goal, everything seems possible [. . .]. Comte wasn't offering anything like that; all he proposed was one's theoretically living on in the memory of mankind [. . .]. Well, that just didn't cut it. (Houellebecq and Lévy 2011, 166)

The trouble with abstract forms of immortality, Houellebecq writes to Lévy, is that "no one gives a shit" (166). Caught up as he was in the ideological fervor surrounding the birth of socialism, Comte was able to celebrate the supposedly incipient demise of monotheism and its promise of personal immortality. The revolutionary enthusiasm of the era afforded Comte the luxury of reveling in God's death, while in Houellebecq's novels all that remains is a sense of postmodern fatalism, the memory of failed utopias, and a persistent, terrifying awareness of looming annihilation.[7]

Comte's thought also informs much of Houellebecq's discussion of rights. The notion of "right" for Comte is a theological construct whose only sanction is in divine will: "The word *right* must be separated from true political language as much as the word *cause* from true philosophical language. Of these two [. . .] notions, the first is [. . .] immoral and anarchic, as the other is irrational and sophistical [. . .]. So long as earthly powers do not emanate from supernatural will, there can exist no real rights" (1968, 361). Without a creator God to affirm them, rights are no more than a shaky human conception subject to the whims of history and human preference—what Comte calls "arbitrary wills" (368). Instead, Comte proclaims that "in the positive state, which no longer admits heavenly titles, the idea of rights disappears irrevocably. Each has his duties, and toward all; but no one has any right" (361). He even goes on to assert that "no one possesses any other right than that of always doing his duty" (361). Rights are therefore to cede to a conception of morality rooted not in metaphysical abstractions or spiritual fictions but in concrete social laws demonstrated through the process of social scientific inquiry: "The necessary superiority of demonstrated morality over revealed morality can therefore be summed up as the definitive substitution of the love of Humanity for the love of God" (356).

The treatment of rights and their moral corollaries follows in the same spirit in Houellebecq's fiction. While the clone narrator of *Particles* derides modern concepts like "personal freedom" and "human dignity" as "confused and arbitrary" (258), the Supreme Sister of *Possibility* dismisses belief in human rights as a simplistic illusion: "Admit that men have neither dignity nor rights; that good and evil are simple notions, scarcely theorized forms of pleasure and pain" (31). Daniel1 takes the Supreme Sister's observation even further, declaring, "As for *human rights*, quite obviously I couldn't give a toss; I could hardly manage to be interested in the rights of my cock" (16). The absence of a discourse of rights does not, however, rule out the existence of moral absolutes, as the reader discovers in the person of young Michel Djerzinski: "reading Nietzsche provoked only a brief irritation, and Kant served only to confirm what he already knew: that perfect morality is unique and universal. Nothing is added to it and nothing changes over the course of time [. . .]. Not determined, it determines; not conditioned, it conditions. It is [. . .] an absolute" (2000a, 28). Houellebecq has recapitulated Djerzinski's point of view in his comments to Lévy:

> The rights of man, human dignity, the foundation of politics, I'm leaving all that aside, I have no theoretical ammunition, nothing that would allow me to validate such standards [. . .]. This leaves ethics, and there, I do have something. Only one thing, to be honest, luminously identified by Schopenhauer, and that is *compassion*. Rightly exalted by Schopenhauer and rightly vilified by Nietzsche as the source of all morality. I sided—and this is hardly news—with Schopenhauer. (2011, 168)

Like Comte, Houellebecq holds out the possibility of establishing a system of morality without divine or metaphysical sanction—that is, without commandments and rights, respectively. "Complete atheists," Houellebecq explains to Lévy, "who are [. . .] convinced of their irremediable mortality, still go on believing in love [and] in moral law and behaving according to its tenets" (145). Following Schopenhauer in his celebration of compassion, rather than reason, as the basis of morality,[8] Houellebecq affirms an innate moral sensibility that exists in the absence of a divine moral absolute.

Finally, Comte and Houellebecq show similarities in their thinking about women and female nature. Where Houellebecq declares, "[I]t seems to me desirable that we should return to a matriarchal society" (Houellebecq 1998, n.p., my translation), Comte writes of women, "This sex is certainly superior to ours regarding the most fundamental attribute of the human species, the tendency to make sociability prevail over personality. In this moral sense [. . .] it deserves our tender veneration, as the purest and most direct instance of Humanity" (1968, 210). Like Fourier, Comte views the ascendancy of women as a supreme indicator of progress, and the veneration of female nature as an important aspect of positivist worship. Houellebecq evokes Comte's view in *The Elementary Particles*, in which Djerzinski muses that "women were indisputably better than men" (137) and that "a world of women would be immeasurably superior" (137). However, the discourse of female superiority in the novel takes an extreme turn in its embrace of the "all-female" society, a notion Houellebecq borrows from the radical feminist thinker Valerie Solanas. In his introduction to the *SCUM Manifesto*, Houellebecq writes,

> For [Solanas] [. . .] woman is not only different, she is *superior.* Biological accident, *femme manquée*, man is an emotional invalid, incapable of concern, compassion, or love for others [. . .]. Man is a monkey armed with a machine gun. In keeping with his violent and selfish nature, in this way he has succeeded in transforming the world, to borrow Valerie's cutting expression, into a "gigantic pile of shit." (2009, 167, my translation)

Houellebecq extends Comte's celebration of the feminine into a parallel condemnation of masculinity and the apparent disaster it has wrought on civilization. For a character such as Djerzinski, the question is no longer one of harmonizing male and female natures, but rather one of suppressing masculinity in order to establish an era of permanent progress.

Numerous other domains exist in which Comte's and Houellebecq's thought follow each other closely, and one could write an entire book detailing the latter's intellectual debt to the former. More generally, however, the greatest commonality between the two writers lies in their sense of historical narrative—which Houellebecq expresses explicitly in *The Elementary Particles* and more implicitly in other works—which identifies the decline of Christianity as the central event of Western modernity. George Chabert writes in reference to *Particles*,

> What [. . .] is the immediate implication of the questioning of Christianity? This is in fact the main subject of Houellebecq's narrative [. . .]. Here is how all this comes together in the course of the centuries: the Enlightenment philosophers deliver a fatal blow to a crisis-stricken Christianity, replacing Christian values with such here-and-now values as freedom and [. . .] equality. Man's value, now circumscribed in his person, releases him from constraining social bonds, facilitating as such the substitution of an agricultural economy with a capitalist economy. Human rights [. . .] are only an alleged ruse of history. With the development of liberal society, man perceives himself more and more powerfully as an *elementary particle.* (2002, 194–95, my translation)

The difference, then, between Comte and Houellebecq is not in their diagnosis of Western malaise, but rather in the confidence each thinker brings to the possibility of a solution to the decline of the Christian worldview.

Like other utopians of his time, Comte expresses great enthusiasm for his remedy to France's spiritual mal de siècle: "Living for others becomes the supreme form of happiness. To incorporate oneself intimately into Humanity, find fellow feeling with past tribulations, sense new destinies, while contributing actively to their realization, will constitute the routine goal of every existence" (1968, 353). Houellebecq, on the other hand, can only mourn the naïveté of such assurance. History has vanquished Christianity, belief in eternal life has buckled beneath the pressure of materialism, and modernity's attempts to create compelling alternatives to the Christian worldview (liberalism, socialism, etc.) have been unable to fill the epistemological breach that God's death has opened. Houellebecq's readers find themselves in profoundly postmodern country, with nothing to guide them except a vague notion of individual freedom that has degraded into a source of permanent anxiety.

Houellebecq can only follow Comte and his nineteenth-century cohort so far, for the fervor surrounding these thinkers' religious or quasi-religious utopianism has vanished in the wake of the twentieth century's great ideological catastrophes. Houellebecq may second Comte's diagnosis of Western malaise, but the hope and excitement that fueled the utopian movements of the nineteenth century elude him. This irreconcilable difference is captured in a memorable scene from *The Map and the Territory*, during which Jed Martin notes the contents of Houellebecq's personal library:

> They went back into the living room to have some coffee. Houellebecq added two logs to the fire, then went away to busy himself in the kitchen. Jed went back to examining the bookcase, and was surprised by the small number of novels—classics, essentially. However, there was an astonishing number of books by social reformers of the nineteenth century: the best known, like Marx, Proudhon, and Comte, but also Fourier, Cabet, Saint-Simon, Pierre Leroux, Owen, Carlyle, as well as others whose names meant almost nothing to him. (2012, 161)

All the great utopian tomes sit peacefully on their shelves, no longer of the slightest utility or interest to contemporary man. Houellebecq has read them all, admired them, and, in the end, consigned them to the cruel verdict of history. As the fictional Houellebecq confesses to Jed, "You know what Comte asserts [. . .] that mankind's dead outnumber the living. Well, I agree with him now. Above all I'm in contact with the dead" (161). The quest for man's salvation in the absence of God is finished. All that remains is to resign oneself to suffering, death, and nothingness.

Abandoned Utopias

If anything is typical of the utopias of Fourier, Saint-Simon, and Comte, it is their total and remarkable failure over the long term. Saint-Simonism expired not long after the death of its leader; the remainder of the sect, led by Barthélemy Prosper Enfantin, was banned in 1832, with the stragglers departing for North Africa and the Middle East in search of new converts. Fourier's influence was less marginal, especially from an intellectual and political point of view, given his affinities with Marxism. But the Fourierist movements that appeared in North America in the mid-nineteenth century, most memorably Brook Farm and the Alphadelphia Association, were some of the more short-lived curiosities of the Second Great Awakening, and what structures remain from those communities are monuments to a forgotten age. Finally, though positivism held some sway in Brazil after the overthrow of the monarchy in 1889, its vestiges linger only in the motto on the Brazilian flag: *Ordem e Progresso.*

The attempts of Fourier, Saint-Simon, and Comte to reform society on religious terms were part of a broader movement to rationalize religion—that is, to make it consonant with the scientific knowledge and social needs of the day. Fourier's system included a virulent reproach of capitalism, and his discourse of "attraction" was clearly linked, however haphazardly, to mechanical principles that had emerged with the birth of modern physics. Saint-Simon and Comte identified theology with social and political corruption and saw it as the product of a primitive, prerational age. Whatever the merit of these judgments, they reflected a broad intuition, born out of the deism of the Enlightenment, that religious knowledge needed to be made consonant with scientific, philosophical, and other advances that occurred in the modern period.

The utopian programs that Houellebecq has embedded in his work can be assigned a place, though with nearly two hundred years of hindsight, in the effort, typical of the French utopian socialists, to elaborate a rational system of religious belief. With this hindsight, however, Houellebecq is forced to take a markedly different tack, and it is no surprise that at the end of *Possibility* (a novel to be read in many respects as the sequel to *Particles*) the reader is led to realize, as Fourier, Saint-Simon, and Comte could not, the futility of this multi-novel utopian program. The narrator of *Particles* has nothing but glowing praise for the clone society encountered at the novel's end: the neohumans, having conquered egotism, cruelty, and anger, are no longer tortured by individual vanity and live the lives of gods in the eyes of their human predecessors (263). Humanity in its former state has all but disappeared, but Houellebecq indicates that this is a happy ending. In *Platform*, however, the robust utopianism of *Particles* begins to wane. The sexual utopia of Eldorador Aphrodite is literally blown to bits by Islamic terrorists, and Michel's lover, Valérie, dies in the attack. Inconsolably bereaved in the wake of this personal apocalypse, Michel can only await death, lamenting having been "a mediocre individual in every possible sense" who does not "deserve anything of [himself] to survive" (258). Subsequently, in *Possibility*, certain neohumans begin to abandon their lives of isolated asceticism, defecting from their compounds in search of a "hypothetical neohuman community" (299) in the Canary Islands. Soon after leaving his compound in Andalusia, Daniel25 remarks,

> My enterprise seemed to me more and more starkly unreasonable, and destined for certain failure [. . .]. I could return, but I had no intention of it: that solitary routine [. . .] which had constituted my life [. . .] now seemed unbearable. Happiness should have come, the happiness felt by good children, guaranteed by the respect of small procedures, by the security that flowed from them [. . .] but happiness had not come, and equanimity had led to torpor [. . .]. The most patent indicator of failure was that I had ended up envying the destiny of Daniel1, his violent and contradictory journey, the amorous passions that had shaken it—whatever his suffering and tragic end. (304–5)

Unlike his preceding incarnations, Daniel25 chooses to abandon a life of asceticism from which there is no foreseeable benefit. Having made a study of Daniel1's life story, he prefers to suffer the misery and despair of his forebear rather than endure the absurdity of an isolated existence. Thus, aware of the dangers of departure but unwilling to return to his previous solitude, he sets out in search of a neohuman community rumored to exist on Lanzarote, the birthplace of Elohimism, where "radical separation [. . .] could be abolished immediately, without waiting for [. . .] the Future Ones" (299).

In the end, however, Daniel25 balks. Having reached the sea after an exhausting journey across the "Great Gray Space" (a flat, featureless desert that was once the ocean floor), Daniel25, "desiccated" (335) on the inside, realizes that neither human nor neohuman life promises him any possibility of happiness. "Organic life [. . .] could not, even if it managed to be reborn, do other than repeat the same patterns: constitution of isolated individuals, predation, selective transmission of the genetic code; nothing new could be expected from it" (334–35). So long as organic life exists, happiness is impossible—hence the neohumans' attempt to transform themselves into biological machines as impervious to suffering as they are to joy. Ultimately, however, biology is to have the last word: "The life of man had been [. . .] dominated by suffering [. . .]. The life of the neohumans was intended to be peaceful, rational, remote from pleasure as well as suffering, and my departure would bear witness to its failure" (329–30).

Embodiment, especially of the carbon-based kind, pushes toward desire and separation, and so long as we remain corporeal beings, happiness eludes us. And yet this sort of existence still strikes Daniel25 as preferable to that of the neohumans, who attempt to elude suffering through a kind of genetically facilitated mortification of the flesh. Caught between these two unappealing forms of life, it is little wonder that Daniel25 elects to live out the rest of his "obscure existence as an improved monkey" (336), as an overgrown amoeba, content to laze thoughtlessly in pools of salt water as his organism imbibes nutrients: "I bathed for a long time under the sun and the starlight, and I felt nothing other than a slightly obscure and nutritive sensation. Happiness was not a possible horizon. The world had betrayed. My body belonged to me for only a brief lapse of time; I would never reach the goal I had set. The future was empty; it was the mountain" (337).

Between desire and sorrow, community and solitude, existence and nonexistence, Daniel25 is able to carve out a narrow space in which his organic functions can persist, a kind of permanent bestial stupefaction, impermeable to thought. I find it difficult to say which of Houellebecq's solutions to existential malaise is more dismal, Daniel25's *abrutissement* or humanity's disappearance. In the latter case the reader is spared the ideological queasiness associated with posthumanism, but in the former Houellebecq indulges in a kind of *prehumanism*, a return to animal brutishness and insensibility whose outcome would hardly be more favorable.

The Possibility of an Island marks the end of Houellebecq's utopian ambitions, at least when considering those utopias that embed a religious clause.

The immortality promised by cloning has led only to boredom and the desire to revert to a previous state, thus signaling a point of closure in Houellebecq's attempts, if only in fiction, to propose an alternative to the religious worldviews that materialism has supposedly eradicated. But this is not the end of the story. *The Map and the Territory*, published after *Possibility*, moves in a surprisingly new direction, implicitly suggesting that the possibilities for utopia lie not in the realm of technological progress but rather, curiously, in the potential economic gain afforded to France by its tourism industry. After spending years secluded on an isolated estate in central France, Jed Martin emerges from his monasticism to find a French countryside that has been transformed by profits from foreign tourists:

> [Jed] had only a vague memory of Châtelus-le-Marcheix. It was, as far as he could remember, a decrepit, ordinary little village in rural France [. . .]. But after his first steps in the streets of the small town, he was filled with amazement. First of all, the village had grown a lot [. . .]. Everywhere on the main street, shop windows were selling regional products and arts and crafts; over one hundred meters he counted three cafés offering low-price Internet connections. [. . .] [T]he departmental council had financed the launch of a geostationary satellite in order to improve the speed of Internet connections in the department. (2012, 260)

In addition to the material prosperity now blessing this formerly isolated and backward part of France, the previous inhabitants of the village have been replaced by educated urbanites eager to exploit the region's tourist potential: "Obviously, France had changed a lot. Incomers, from urban areas, had replaced them, motivated by a real appetite for business and, occasionally, by moderate and marketable ecological convictions. They had set about repopulating the *hinterland*—and this attempt, after many other fruitless attempts, based this time on a precise knowledge of the laws of the market, and on their lucid acceptance, had been a total success" (261). In this image of an economically renewed France, the suffocating hegemony of the état providence has disappeared, capitalism has finally managed to overcome the entrenched welfare state, and the country has been turned into what Houellebecq refers to in *Public Enemies* as a "tourist brothel" (Houellebecq and Lévy, 2011, 117). The focusing of commerce on tourism and the countryside has put an end to industrial production in France, thus prompting a steep decline in immigration and the insecurity often associated with it. Of France's newfound economic prosperity, Houellebecq writes: "Having become a mainly agricultural and tourist country, France had displayed remarkable robustness during the various crises which followed one another [. . .] in the preceding twenty years [. . .]. Having scarcely anything to sell except *hôtels de charme*, perfumes, and *rillettes*—what is called an *art de vivre*—France had no difficulty confronting these vagaries" (2012, 262). And apropos of the effects of the end of immigration and the welfare state: "This new generation turned out to be more conservative and more respectful of money and social hierarchies [. . .]. The birth rate had [. . .] actually risen in France, even without taking into account immigration, which, anyway, had fallen to almost zero since the disappearance of the last industrial jobs and the drastic reduction of social security coverage" (263).

And so France is cured of all its current ills: the unaffordable welfare state, burdensome immigration and the dangers of Islamicization, the social atomization provoked by antipathy between the generations, the environmental hazards of industrial production, and the financial insolvency of a population with a declining birth rate. This is a veritable materialist utopia—though one much more likely to appeal, I suppose, to the French right. Otherwise, the emphasis on the economic exploitation of the French countryside and on the image of France's more traditional past (Belle Époque furnishings, country hotels, luxury products, etc.) is not purely of Houellebecq's invention. Gilles Lipovetsky, one of France's most eminent theorists of postmodernity, describes the trend in his 2004 essay *Hypermodern Times* (*Les temps hypermodernes*), writing of the commercial value of France's cultural heritage, "The vogue of the past can also be read in the success of antiques, fine china, retro, *vintage*, products stamped 'authentic' that inspire nostalgia. More and more, businesses refer to their history, exploit their heritage, invoke the past, launch 'memory products' that 'bring back to life' former times [. . .]. In hypermodern society, the old and the nostalgic have become selling points, marketing tools" (86, my translation).

The Map and the Territory imagines a France that has become keenly aware of its cultural heritage and natural beauty and has learned to exploit its past in order to guarantee its economic future. Utopianism exists in a material sense—France has survived the collapse of industrial and financial capitalism by concentrating its economy on a sort of "capitalism of the countryside," able to withstand the vicissitudes of the global market—suggesting a more modest attempt on Houellebecq's part to remedy the perceived woes of modernity, be they spiritual, existential, or economic. Gone is the preoccupation with immortality that formed the utopian firmament of much of Houellebecq's previous work; gone too is any mention of the existential burdens of godlessness and disbelief. Has Houellebecq embraced materialism, in both its philosophical and market senses? Or has he subtly suggested, by placing France's hopes for redemption in a return to tradition (if only for the purposes of profit), that spiritual renewal might too depend on a reinvestment and rejuvenation of France's religious past?

It would be difficult to deny that a "return to tradition" in the French sense would also connote some rehabilitation of Catholicism as a socially-structuring institution. Catholicism is one of the principal jurisdictions of France's cultural heritage (one has only to visit the cathedral at Chartres to realize this), and Houellebecq's evocation of a "more conservative" generation of French men and women who are more respectful than ever before of the social order seems almost to demand some mention of a reawakening interest in the Catholic Church. France, after all, saw hopes for a Catholic renaissance, both in literature and in culture more generally, come and go in the late nineteenth century and early twentieth, attracting some of the most renowned novelists and intellectuals of the time. Figures including J.-K. Huysmans, François Coppée, Ferdinand Brunnetière, and Adolphe Retté produced novels, memoirs, and essays recounting their experiences of conversion, their antipathy toward contemporary individualism and materialism, and their nostalgia for a lost golden age of faith (the Middle Ages) that contrasted in the most gross manner with the modern world.[9] The era also saw the appearance of "digest versions" relating the various stages of the cross and the ultimate conversion of prominent intellectuals, while others offered compilations of the best Catholic writing of the time.

Works such as Jean Calvet's *Le renouveau catholique dans la littérature contemporaine* (1927) and Jules Sageret's *Les grands convertis* (1906) explore the spiritual preoccupations and conversion experiences of Huysmans, Paul Bourget, Coppée, and Brunnetière, while Louis Chaigne's *Anthologie de la renaissance catholique* (1940) anthologizes poetry by Charles Péguy, Paul Claudel, François Mauriac, and others. Frédéric Gugelot describes the worldview typical of these "great converts": "The historical vision of the converts developed a total refusal of the society issuing from the Renaissance, the Reformation, and the revolution of 1789. This rejection was strengthened by hatred of a time dominated by individualism, rationalism and the secularization of thought and of the state. Nostalgia for the Middle Ages participated in this intransigence toward the contemporary world" (1998, 394, my translation). In his widely celebrated 1897 book, *La bonne souffrance*, François Coppée offers a glimpse of the enthusiasm that attended expectations for a Catholic renaissance in France: "Official atheism must resign itself. We are beginning to abandon these schools of falsehood, where there is nothing for the heart. We are finally realizing that they are populating France with the prideful and the desperate, and, from all quarters, brilliant signs allow us to presage a victorious Renaissance of the Christian Idea" (224–25, my translation).

The Houellebecquian critique of contemporary culture's reckless individualism, heartless rationalism, and unchecked secularism not only echoes but shares in the essential spirit of the Catholic intellectuals of a century or more past. The death of God is only shortly followed by the death of France; no society can sustain itself on atheism, no matter how imbued with the humanistic spirit, and France, along with all of the West, stands on a precipice from which only supernatural succor can save it. Could it then be that Houellebecq, in *The Map and the Territory,* has dared to imagine, if only in the subtlest way, a Catholic renaissance for the twenty-first century, in which a return to economic and social traditionalism will be accompanied by a swelling of interest in a previously neglected and nearly obsolete Catholicism?

The answer is both yes and no. Curiously, conversion in *The Map and the Territory* is limited to the fictional Houellebecq, who chooses to be baptized not long after he moves back to his childhood home in the Loire Valley and not long before his gruesome murder: "It had been discovered, to everyone's surprise, that the author of *The Elementary Particles*, who throughout his life had displayed an intransigent atheism, had very discreetly been baptized, in a church in Courtenay, six months before [his death]" (202). Houellebecq's conversion is not, however, depicted in any sense as part of a more general trend toward a return to Catholicism; more than anything else, Parisian church officials use it during Houellebecq's funeral as a means of proselytizing (202), having resorted to exploiting the deaths of celebrities as a "disheartening solution" to the "regular progress of atheism" (202). *The Map and the Territory* thus merely hints at the Catholic renaissance that writers such as Coppée and Retté imagine in more certain terms.

By linking the fictional Houellebecq's conversion with a return to his "ancestral home" in Loiret, the novel suggests a connection between the rehabilitation of France's countryside and its traditions and the religious life that used to animate them. "However freely they mock," writes Somerset Maugham in *The Razor's Edge*, "most Frenchmen, when the end comes, prefer to make their peace with the faith that is part of their blood and bones" (1944, 255). Does the future French society of *The Map and the Territory* prefer to make such a peace? Houellebecq does not say either way, and certainly the mention of the "regular progress of atheism" (202) shows that Houellebecq is still writing within a secularizing paradigm. However, what this very cautious overture to Catholicism does accomplish is to move us away from the techno-utopianism encountered in previous works and to place the question of religious revival in the context of extant faith traditions. *The Map and the Territory* represents a rupture with the techno-religious discourse of *The Elementary Particles* and *The Possibility of an Island*, leaving the door open for a more traditionally religious solution to contemporary existential malaise. In this respect, the novel serves as a bridge between the utopian disappointments of Houellebecq's previous texts and the triumph of Islam in *Submission*.

Materialist Horror

The world outside had its own rules, and those rules were not human.

—Houellebecq 2000a

As I have argued throughout, Houellebecq's novels may in large part be read as tales of the social and psychological consequences of a thoroughly materialist worldview. Without God, transcendence, or sacredness to guide them, Houellebecq's characters all too often abandon themselves to hedonistic perversions, wither away in isolation from the rest of humanity, or commit suicide. Love and art do at times play a redeeming role; one might consider the belated relationship between Michel and Annabelle in *Particles*, which sustains them both for a time, or the artistic success that allows Jed in *The Map and the Territory* to attain a state of mind that, while "joyless," is nonetheless "peaceful" and "completely neutral" (167). The redemption that love and art might provide is, however, fleeting: Annabelle's death is a grim reminder of nature's indifference to human concerns, while Jed's final art project—a series of videos in which human beings are devoured by plants—is a resolutely Houellebecquian display of apocalyptic horror.

Houellebecq is an author who "glimpses the end in everything," as the late French novelist and cultural critic

Philippe Muray pointed out in his 1999 review of *The Elementary Particles*. And that end, whatever form it takes, always reflects a kind of horror about the human condition, a sense that, whatever temporary reprieve humanity may discover from the inconveniences of organic life, we are all nonetheless doomed to stink and rot, with no God to save us. The horror of Houellebecq's novels is thus a materialist horror, the product of an experimental approach to literature in which a distraught and defenseless humanity is relentlessly confronted with the inexorabilities of material existence and the indifference of the natural world. The following passage from *H. P. Lovecraft: Against the World, Against Life* describing the Lovecraftian universe might just as well be a summary of Houellebecq's method:

> Of course, life has no meaning. But neither does death. And that is another thing that curdles the blood when one discovers Lovecraft's universe. The deaths of his heroes have no meaning. Death brings no appeasement. It in no way allows the story to conclude. Implacably, HPL destroys his characters, evoking only the dismemberment of marionettes. Indifferent to these pitiful vicissitudes, cosmic fear continues to expand. It swells and takes form. Great Cthulhu emerges from his slumber. (2005, 32)

In the following section, focusing in particular on *Whatever*, I present what are, in my view, some of the most exemplary instances of materialist horror in Houellebecq's fiction. However, I want to insist that such instances represent, precisely, horror stories, and like all horror stories their purchase on reality is only partial. The value of such writing lies not so much in conveying the real as in reminding us of the desperate places our intellectual and spiritual commitments may take us in the worst of circumstances—circumstances like physical decline, disease, ugliness, abandonment, rejection, and death. Houellebecq prompts his readers to consider the stakes involved in the renunciation of God, of the soul, and of transcendence, even if he has very little to place in their stead.

Dangerous Credibility

One of the most persistent themes in *Whatever* (1994), Houellebecq's debut novel, is human ugliness. Three characters in particular find themselves burdened by a repulsive appearance: Raphaël Tisserand, the narrator's partner during a business trip, who looks like a "frog in formaldehyde" (2011, 98); Catherine Lechardoy, the narrator's liaison at the French Ministry of Agriculture, who is "beyond trying it on with a man" (26); and the pitiful and ironically named Brigitte Bardot, a sort of metafictional character whom we encounter in one of the novel's animal fictions, who has the aspect of a "sow" (87).

Houellebecq is systematically unsparing in his depiction of each of these unfortunate souls' physical loathsomeness, using language that evokes not only the arbitrariness of nature but also the indifference of the Ultimate. Of Lechardoy, he writes, "She's not all that pretty. As well as prominent teeth she has lifeless hair, little eyes that burn with anger. No breasts or buttocks to speak of. God has not, in truth, been too kind to her" (26). Obviously there is no question of this middling office worker having anything like a sex life. At a meeting between the narrator and several representatives from the ministry, during which the two parties are to lay out a plan for teaching a "specialized software" (15) to employees in the countryside, the narrator observes: "The third Ministry representative is Catherine Lechardoy. The poor thing has a slightly sad air this morning [. . .]. Her ugly little face is glum, she regularly wipes her glasses. I even wonder if she hasn't been crying; I can just picture her breaking into sobs in the morning as she gets dressed, all alone" (33). If this were not bad enough, when the narrator briefly considers coming on to Catherine during an office party, he becomes physically ill:

> After my third glass I came close to suggesting we leave together, go and fuck in some office; on the desk or on the carpet, it didn't matter; I was feeling up to making the necessary gestures. But I kept my mouth shut; and anyway I don't think she'd have accepted; or else I'd have first had to put my arm around her waist, say she was beautiful, brush her lips in a tender kiss. There was no way out, for sure. I briefly excused myself and went to throw up in the toilets. (45)

During the narrator's absence, Catherine returns to the party and is seen "listening [. . .] docilely" (45) to one of the ministry's theoreticians: "She'd managed, in short, to regain control; perhaps it was all to the good, for her" (45).

Lechardoy's ugliness is a precursor to that of Raphaël Tisserand. Houellebecq describes Tisserand's futility in matters of seduction and sex in the most categorical terms. While on a train from Paris to Rouen to begin teaching his software courses, the narrator remarks apropos of his partner: "Vaguely Mediterranean in type, he is certainly rather fat [. . .] added to which his baldness is coming along nicely [. . .]. He has the exact appearance of a buffalo toad—thick, gross, heavy, deformed features, the very opposite of handsome. His shiny acned skin seems to permanently exude a greasy fluid. He wears bifocal glasses, because he's extremely near-sighted to boot" (54). As the story moves forward, the narrator several times witnesses Tisserand's failure to draw the slightest interest from the women he attempts to seduce. After drinking too much one evening at a bar full of students, Tisserand is "totally haggard. Wordlessly he lets me pay the bill, wordlessly he follows me as I make for the door. He's stooped, huddled; he's ashamed of himself, hates himself, wishes he were dead" (64). Tisserand's despair reaches such depths that during a night out at a dance club on the Atlantic coast, the narrator tries to convince his colleague to murder two adolescents who have left the discotheque to fornicate on the beach. Speaking about women in general, the narrator enjoins Tisserand,

> It's not their beauty [that is most precious about them], I can tell you that much; it isn't their vagina either, nor even their love; because all these disappear with life itself. And from now on you can possess their life. Launch yourself on a career of murder this very evening [. . .]. When you feel these women trembling at the end of your knife [. . .] then you will truly be the master; then will you possess them body and soul [. . .]. A knife, Raphaël, is a powerful ally. (116–17)

Things take a turn toward the burlesque, however, and instead of stabbing his potential victims, Tisserand ends up masturbating as the woman fellates the man: "I turned back, I walked between the dunes. I could have killed them; they were oblivious to everything, they didn't even know I was there. I masturbated. I had no wish to kill them; blood changes nothing" (120). Tisserand then speeds off back to Paris, only to be killed along the way when his car is crushed by a big rig: "I was never to see Tisserand again; he was killed in his car that night, on his return trip to Paris [. . .]. His 205 GTI collided head-on with a lorry that had pulled out into the middle of the carriageway. He died instantly, just before dawn" (120). At twenty-eight years old, Tisserand has ended his life a virgin. The novel reports the news of his death so abruptly that the reader cannot help recalling Houellebecq's description of Lovecraft's universe, where the "deaths of his heroes have no meaning," and "[d]eath brings no appeasement"—all of it "evoking only the dismemberment of marionettes." Houellebecq writes: "Around ten we learn of the death of Tisserand. A call from the family which a secretary passes on to the whole staff. We will receive, she says, a formal announcement later. I can't really believe it; it's too nightmarish for words. But no, it's all true" (129).

However nightmarish the tale of Raphaël Tisserand may be, Houellebecq nonetheless reserves the bulk of his rhetorical violence for Brigitte Bardot, an obese adolescent with "no girlfriends" and "obviously no boyfriends" who is "completely alone" in her sixth-form class (87). Bardot appears in the somewhat bizarre context of the narrator's animal fictions, specifically in a work entitled *Dialogues Between a Dachshund and a Poodle* (83), wherein one of the dogs "is reading aloud, to his companion, a manuscript found in the roll-top desk of his young master" (83–84). The canine narrator tells of Bardot,

> Brigitte Bardot was truly repulsive. First of all she was extremely fat, a porker and even a super-porker, with abundant rolls of fat gracelessly disposed at the intersections of her obese body. Yet had she followed a slimming diet of the most frightening severity for twenty-five years her fate would not have been markedly improved. Because her skin was blotchy, puffy and acned. And her face was wide, flat and round, with little deep-set eyes, and straggly, lusterless hair. Indeed, the comparison with a sow forced itself on everyone. (87)

All is not lost for Bardot, however, for the writer of the manuscript appears to take pity on her—a pity mixed, naturally, with a sort of zoological fascination that is typically Houellebecquian: "Her hormonal mechanisms must have functioned normally, there's no reason to suppose otherwise. And then? Does that suffice for having erotic fantasies? Did she imagine masculine hands lingering between the folds of her obese belly? Descending as far as her sexual parts? I turn to medicine and medicine can afford me no answer. There are many things concerning Bardot that I have not managed to elucidate. I have tried" (87–88).

In an attempt to discover those answers that medicine apparently cannot afford, the story's narrator takes to talking with Bardot during class—nothing resembling a conversation, but rather requests for explanations about math problems, for example, and "all this with great prudence" (88–89). He even goes so far as to "touch her hand, in a seemingly accidental way," to which Brigitte reacts "as if to an electric shock," and the effect produced is "rather impressive" (89). Things continue in this way for a few weeks, and "the culminating point of our relations was attained just before Christmas, when I again accompanied her to her train [. . .]. That evening, in the middle of the platform, I kissed her on the cheek" (89). But fearing he has been spotted by another student, the narrator stops speaking to Brigitte after the Christmas holidays. He then reflects that "dating Bardot would have demanded a moral strength far superior to the one I could [. . .] pride myself on. Because not only was she ugly but she was plain nasty. Goaded on by sexual liberation [. . .] she couldn't make appeal to some ethical notion of virginity, obviously. On top of that she was too intelligent and too lucid to account for her state as being a product of "Judeo-Christian influence [. . .]. All means of evasion were thus closed to her" (89–90). The narrator is not unaware of the cruel nature of his experiment with Bardot—an experiment that seems to have been aimed not so much at comforting her, but rather at accounting for the existence of her otherwise normal human consciousness within such an aberrantly repugnant physical form. He explains:

> In the end I am not terribly proud of this story. The whole thing was too manifestly ludicrous to be devoid of cruelty. For example I recall myself greeting her one morning with these words, "Oh, you have a new dress, Brigitte." It was really repulsive, even if true; because the fact is amazing but nonetheless real: *she'd changed her dress*. I even remember one time when she'd put *a ribbon in her hair*: Oh my God! a calf's head decorated with chopped parsley, more like. I implore her pardon in the name of all humanity. (90)

One would have an easy enough time reproaching such descriptions for their cruelty, and, were it not for the fact that the absolute, irremediable, and even imponderable ugliness of a character like Bardot might seem comic in its excess and incongruity, such rhetorical insensitivity would likely fail to dismay only the most cynical of readers. The journalist Marie-Françoise Colombani, whom Houellebecq quotes in *Public Enemies*, writes apropos of *Platform*, "You have to keep telling yourself it isn't true, life isn't like this, that it's like some horrid story you might tell children[;] you have to read this book the way we play at scaring ourselves" (Houellebecq and Lévy 2011, 275).

Colombani's remark goes right to the heart of materialist horror: however terse and "realist" in tone Houellebecq's novels might be, such realism is in fact a cleverly wrought delivery mechanism for disproportionate and surreal horror.

It is helpful to consider, for the sake of argument, the numerous and rather obvious objections to the claim that Houellebecq's fiction should be assimilated to a kind of "social realism" tracking the demise of moral and spiritual values in a secular, late capitalist West.[1] For example, while the ugliness of a creature like Tisserand is certainly believable enough (and one cannot help feeling legitimate pity when he describes himself as "a shrink-wrapped chicken leg on a supermarket shelf"; 98), many readers no doubt have difficulty accepting the notion that characters like Tisserand, Lechardoy, and Bardot would be forced to endure the sexual pauperization that Houellebecq's novels take to be their lot. In *Whatever*, Tisserand is concerned with trying to seduce young—college- or even high-school-aged—girls, who are young enough that they may be prone to reject him for reasons other than his appearance. Never does Houellebecq mention the possibility that Tisserand might date someone his own age or someone *of his own looks*; his sexual failures come off as the result not so much of universal rejection, but rather of his feverish attempts to play out of his league. Why not have Tisserand date Catherine Lechardoy, for example? Surely these two would not be so repulsed by each other that they would in all instances refuse each other's intimacy. Experience does not confirm *Whatever*'s thesis about sexual pauperization. The great majority of people *do* eventually find a bedmate; the person may not be particularly attractive—he or she might even be "plain nasty," as Houellebecq writes of Bardot—but the fact that such people exist indicates that a set of equally unprepossessing parents conspired to conceive them. Understood most cynically, *Whatever*'s theory of sexual pauperization represents a complaint by average-looking, somewhat aging men about their inability to gain sexual favors from nubile adolescents. The novel's main thesis, read in a certain light, winds up sounding like a declaration of erotic snobbery proffered by those unwilling to lower standards to which they themselves no longer, or never did, live up.

A similar complaint appears in *Platform*, a novel that condemns a putative "erotic laxity" on the part of contemporary Europeans. Houellebecq writes,

> Offering your body as an object of pleasure, giving pleasure unselfishly: that's what westerners don't know how to do anymore.

> They've completely lost the sense of giving. Try as they might, they no longer feel sex as something *natural* [. . .]. We have become cold, rational, acutely conscious of our individual existence and our rights; more than anything, we want to avoid alienation and dependence; on top of that, we're obsessed with health and hygiene. These are hardly ideal conditions in which to make love. (2002, 174–75)

Some validity certainly exists in these observations. It would be hard to deny, for example, that the proliferation of pornography, especially through the Internet, has produced, or at least suggested, physical standards that may not have applied in the past. Likewise, experience shows that with an increase in sexual partners, relationships, and other liaisons, the ability to feel sentimental abandon tends to decrease. People become wary of being rejected, sick of suffering, and the adolescent tendency to throw oneself heart and soul at a person is very naturally replaced by a more cautious approach. To the extent that individual liberty can lead to sexual profligacy, one can reasonably infer some link between the acute consciousness of our individual existence and a reluctance to place ourselves in a state of dependency vis-à-vis a romantic partner.

Difficult, however, to countenance in this passage is the hardly veiled insinuation that contemporary Westerners are somehow no longer enjoying having sex with each other. Such a claim seems wholly out of line with common sense: good or bad sex depends mostly on the person with whom one engages in it, not on the civilization to which one belongs. Even more important to note is that the sexual ideal that Houellebecq's novels enshrine—in which lovers abandon themselves to each other's affections—is less an indictment of Western sexual mores and more a championing of a very adolescent vision of romantic experience. The ability to throw caution to the wind in matters of romance is the luxury of those who have not suffered rejection, deceit, or betrayal, and while one might be jealous of those who remain in such a state of naïveté, the inevitability of its being shattered leads one more often than not to feelings of pity at the thought of lost innocence. Houellebecq's fiction does not consider that the experience of amorous disappointment might lead to a person's psychological maturation, and with that the possibility of founding a future relationship on something more stable than mere sentimental abandon. Rather, Houellebecq offers a vision of the romantic in which "love as a kind of innocence and as a capacity for illusion, as an aptitude for epitomizing the whole of the other sex in a single loved being rarely resists a year of sexual immorality, and never two" (2011, 113); that is, disappointment, temporary cynicism, and experimentation render a person not the wiser for the wear, but instead permanently incapable of love. It is a horrifying statement; certainly, most sexually mature people have lost, or simply curtailed out of the wisdom of repeated experience, that capacity for abandon that Houellebecq identifies as necessary for "love."

Many of Houellebecq's theses thus fail to bear scrutiny, rendering problematic the claims that Houellebecq's fiction is, as John McCann has argued, a "reflection of the social and economic reality of contemporary life" (2011, 1). This is not to say that Houellebecq is not deeply contemporary; the trouble, rather, is that Houellebecq's modus operandi as a novelist is experimental rather than realist (realism being understood here in the ontological rather than stylistic sense), and thus the interest in evaluating his work lies in whether the results of the experiment are intelligible in contemporary terms, not whether they describe contemporary conditions. The cases of Tisserand, Lechardoy, and Bardot, for example, ought at the very least lead one to reflect on the injustices that matter seems arbitrarily to inflict on human beings, as well as on the ways in which modern liberalism and its propaganda arm, advertising, insists on and thereby inflates these natural injustices. Likewise, Michel's tirade against Western sexuality in *Platform*, however implausible in many ways, stirs up important questions about the relationships among individualism, narcissism, sexuality, and the changes in sexual values that followed the upheaval of the 1960s. So long as the reader agrees to play by the rules of his experiment, Houellebecq has much to say about the dangers of unfettered scientism, secularization, the commodification of sexuality, and the narcissism that may grow out of excessive individualism. Whatever exaggeration or error may be involved in these renderings is beside the point. What matters is whether the results of the experiment are convincing *within the parameters laid forth*. That is, the results need not be culturally accurate; they need only be culturally intelligible, and the careful reader will separate truth from falsity, insight from excess.

For the remainder of this chapter, I explore the origins of the concept of "materialist horror" as Houellebecq wields it, first by drawing several parallels between Lovecraft's texts and Houellebecq's, and then by examining a link with Blaise Pascal, whom Houellebecq has often cited as an influence. The connection with Lovecraft becomes apparent through a consideration of the theme of humanity's insignificance in the greater cosmic scheme; the relation with Pascal emerges through an examination of the authors' shared sensitivity to the terror of the infinite.

Lovecraft, Pascal, Houellebecq

The American horror fiction writer Howard Phillips Lovecraft is today best known for his creation of the Cthulhu mythos, a series of weird stories, including "The Call of Cthulhu," *At the Mountains of Madness*, and *The Shadow Out of Time*, which have inspired the artist H. R. Giger and the imagery of the *Alien* film series; global heavy metal icon Metallica; and contemporary horror fiction writers, including Stephen King. Lovecraft, a highborn New Englander who died poor and unrecognized in 1937, was a famous misanthrope, and his cycle of Cthulhu stories demonstrates a sensitivity to the insignificance of humanity's place in the universe that few modern writers have matched. *The Shadow Out of Time*, for example, a tale in which a New England professor named Peaslee trades bodies with a Yithian and is sent millions of years into the past to live among this erstwhile race, reveals an eons-old cosmology of innumerable galactic civilizations compared with which human life appears only as an afterthought. Lovecraft writes,

> After man there would be a mighty beetle civilization, the bodies of whose members the cream of the Great Race would seize when the monstrous doom overtook the elder world. Later, as the earth's span closed, the transferred minds would again migrate through time and space—to another stopping-place in the bulbous vegetable entities of Mercury. But there would be races after them, clinging pathetically to the cold planet and burrowing its horror filled core, before the utter end. (2009, 288–89)

The Lovecraft scholar S. T. Joshi offers a summary of Lovecraftian cosmology: "Lovecraft, in a major departure from the previous horror tradition [. . .] would emphasize the insignificance of humanity in a universe that appears to be boundless both in space and time. He would do this chiefly by the depiction of immense entities—called 'gods' by human beings who cannot comprehend such creatures except by appeals to a deity—from the farthest depths of space" (2008, xi). Cthulhu, Azathoth, Yog-Sothoth—readers of Lovecraft will recognize these names as the horrible, inhuman superbeings that lie just beyond the reaches of known time and space, awaiting the proper invocations and magical utterances in order to loose their fury on humankind. Confronted with these blasphemous entities, Lovecraft's characters—a series of invariably dour male academicians—dangle on the cusp of madness, unable completely to accept yet also unable to deny the enormity of the terrible cosmic mysteries they have glimpsed. "I shall never sleep calmly again," confesses the protagonist of "The Call of Cthulhu," Francis Wayland Thurston, after having come nearly face to face with Cthulhu through the harrowing account of a Norwegian ship captain, "when I think of the horrors that lurk ceaselessly behind life in time and space, and of those unhallowed blasphemies from elder stars which dream beneath the sea, known and favored by a nightmare cult ready and eager to loose them on the world whenever another earthquake shall heave their monstrous stone city again to the sun and air" (Lovecraft 2008, 375).

Particularly notable about the Cthulhu mythos is the utter absence of any supernatural quality in the assortment of monsters, aliens, and other hideously described organisms that the reader discovers in Lovecraft's tales. Joshi writes, "Lovecraft was, above all else, a scientific rationalist. His tales appear to put on stage a bewildering array of outlandish monsters [. . .] but Lovecraft, as his letters attest, was a materialist and an atheist who had the highest respect for scientific fact and who saw nothing but pitiable folly in the delusions of religion, spiritualism, and occultism" (2008, xiii). The materialism of Lovecraft's cosmology is not lost on Houellebecq. In his introduction to *H. P. Lovecraft: Against the World, Against Life*, Houellebecq writes,

> It is possible, in fact, that beyond the narrow range of our perception, other entities exist [. . .]. But this is not necessarily good news. What makes us think that these creatures [. . .] will exhibit any kind of a *spiritual* nature? There is nothing to suggest a transgression of the universal laws of egotism and malice. It is ridiculous to imagine that at the edge of the cosmos, other well-intentioned and wise beings await to guide us toward some sort of harmony. In order to imagine how they might treat us were we to come into contact with them, it might be best to recall how we treat "inferior intelligences" such as rabbits and frogs. In the best of cases they serve as *food* for us; sometimes also, often in fact, we kill them for the sheer pleasure of killing. (2005, 33)

The horror of Lovecraft's fiction, eloquently expressed in Houellebecq's account, lies in its evocation of a despiritualized cosmos, where galactic powers stand in the same relation to humanity as humanity stands to "lower" animals like rodents and amphibians. Cosmic fear emerges when man beholds, if only elusively, the immense, alien forces of nature that rule the universe; and his only chance of sanity lies in his ignorance of them. As Thurston elaborates at the beginning of "The Call of Cthulhu,"

> The most merciful thing in the world, I think, is the inability of the human mind to correlate its contents. We live on a placid island of ignorance in the midst of black seas of infinity, and it was not meant that we should voyage far. The sciences, each straining in its own direction, have hitherto harmed us little; but some day the piecing together of dissociated knowledge will open up such terrifying vistas of reality, and of our frightful position therein, that we shall either go mad from the revelation or flee from the deadly light into the peace and safety of a new dark age. (Lovecraft 2008, 354)

Houellebecq's characters do not exactly occupy the "placid island of ignorance" for which Thurston pines, scientific knowledge having already stripped protagonists like Djerzinski, Bruno, Michel, and Daniel1 of the theological assurances of a putative golden age of faith. In Houellebecq's novels, cosmic fear is already complete (assuming, of course, that one allows for the absence of alien monsters from the depths of space), and no hope exists of a flight into the "peace and safety of a new dark age." An intuition of humanity's threatened existence, of an end to the human through either extinction or replacement (or both), forms an essential component of the psychology of Houellebecq's protagonists. Near the finale of *The Elementary Particles*, Houellebecq describes Djerzinski and Annabelle's doomed relationship:

> They sometimes were sad, but mostly they were serious. Both of them knew that this would be their last human relationship, and this feeling lacerated every moment they spent together. They had a great respect and profound sympathy for each other, and there were days when, caught up in some sudden magic, they knew moments of fresh air and glorious, bracing sunshine. For the most part, however, they could feel a gray shadow moving over them, on the earth that supported them, and in everything they could glimpse the end. (197)

The "gray shadow" moving over the earth in Lovecraft's cosmology is Great Cthulhu, who awakens from an eons-old slumber at the bottom of the sea to once again bring the planet under his spell. In Houellebecq's novels the shadow is the less cosmic but no less horrible certainty of death and nothingness, and only through Djerzinski's discoveries in genetics at the end of *Particles* will Annabelle's death come to have any meaning. What Houellebecq and Lovecraft share most is their sensitivity to the fleetingness of the human in view of the broader forces of nature that determine our destiny, be those forces agential, as in the case of aliens, or mechanical, as with physical law. Near the end of *Particles*, Annabelle is diagnosed with uterine cancer and undergoes a hysterectomy: "After the third week she was allowed out, and would take short walks along the river or in the surrounding woods [. . .]. The grass on the riverbank was scorched, almost white; in the shadow of the beech trees, the river wound on forever in deep green ripples. The world outside had its own rules, and those rules were not human" (228–29). The evil agency of Lovecraft's monsters is transformed in Houellebecq's fiction into the indifferent though no less inhuman agency of an arbitrary nature, which visits sickness and death on humanity without any need of intelligent outside forces and which for this reason may be even more horrifying. Houellebecq and Lovecraft not only succeed in conveying the fleetingness of human life in the larger theater of nature, they also effect a memorable and frightful demonstration of human beings' helplessness in the face of an inhuman otherness, be it cosmic or terrestrial.

In some ways, Houellebecq is Lovecraft sans the ornate cosmology of ageless creatures and ancient races. Only in the clones of *The Possibility of an Island* does the reader confront anything resembling the cosmic powers inhabiting Lovecraft's universe; and the clones' indifference to the welfare of the human race—the "human savages" in *Possibility*—is perhaps on a par with that of the Yithians and the Great Old Ones of the Lovecraftian weird tales.[2] Daniel24, for instance, admits in his life story to feeling "no pity" for or "sense of common belonging" (18) with the savages roaming the countryside at the outset of the fifth millennium. While he will leave his compound in order to rescue an injured dog or rabbit, the idea of helping a human being is unthinkable. Daniel24's indifference to humanity thus approaches that of a Yog-Sothoth or Cthulhu, and offers perhaps the clearest parallel with Lovecraft's fiction in Houellebecq's work.

Nonetheless, Lovecraft's oft-deplored bombast and endless parade of extravagant, extraterrestrial monsters make too strict a comparison of him and Houellebecq problematic. Lovecraft, as Houellebecq points out in *H. P. Lovecraft: Against the World, Against Life*, wants very much to go beyond the human, to eschew realism and enliven the monotony of the day-to-day with unholy rites, gruesome murders, and cosmic horrors beyond description (29). Houellebecq's approach is more often than not rooted in the mundane lives of characters whose only escape from ennui and angst lies in television, midline consumer products, sex, and regular visits to the neighborhood Monoprix.[3] The roots of materialist horror sink deeper than Lovecraft's fiction and, I argue, are better traced to the seventeenth-century French philosopher and mathematician Blaise Pascal and the proto-cosmology of the *Pensées*.

Of the many memorable thoughts contained in the *Pensées* (the most philosophically enduring no doubt being number 680, the famed "wager" argument), pensée 230 is perhaps the most significant in relation to Houellebecq. In this lengthy discourse on the "disproportion of man," Pascal asks, "What is man in infinity?" (1995, 66)—both the infinitely large and the infinitesimally small, the infinity of limitless space and of the eternally contracting microcosm of the atomic (and subatomic) world. Of space, Pascal writes,

> Let the earth appear a pinpoint to us beside the vast arc this star describes, and let us be dumbfounded that this vast arc is itself only a delicate pinpoint in comparison with the arc encompassed by the stars tracing circles in the firmament. But if our vision stops here, let our imagination travel further afield. Our imagination will grow weary of conceiving before nature of producing. The whole of the visible world is merely an imperceptible speck in nature's ample bosom [. . .]. (1995, 66)

And of the inconceivably minute,

> Let us see in [this miniature atom] an infinity of universes, of which each has its own firmament, planets, and earth in the same proportion as in the visible world, in this land of animals, and ultimately of mites, in which we will find the same thing as in the first universe, and will find again in others the same thing, endlessly and perpetually. Let us lose ourselves in these wonders, which are as startling in their minuteness as others are in the vastness of their size. (67)

Instead of wonder, however, man's knowledge of his intermediate nature—a being occupying an ontological space somewhere between the atom and the galaxy—leads to a sense of terror: "Whoever looks at himself in this way will be terrified by himself, and, thinking himself supported by the size nature has given us suspended between the two gulfs of the infinite and the void, will tremble at nature's wonders" (67). Even Pascal, a man of great faith, is frightened by the sheer scope of nature: "The eternal silence of these infinite spaces terrifies me" (73). Humanity's only solace in the face of cosmic immensity and atomic minuteness—in a world where "what we have of being hides from us the knowledge of the first principles which emerge from nothingness," but where "the scant being we have hides from us the sight of infinity" (69)—is our ability to think: "All our dignity consists therefore in thought. It is from there that we must be lifted up and not from space and time, which we could never fill" (73). Because man is a "thinking reed" (72), he is nobler than the universe: man "knows that he is dying" (73) and that "the universe has an advantage over him" (73). But the universe "knows nothing about this" (73), and thus through thought—and in Pascal's case, the sort of thought leading to Christian faith—man can overcome his disadvantage and escape being swallowed up by infinity through the act of joining his being to an infinite creator.

What Pascal offers in pensée 230 is a cosmology of liminality: a view of humanity's place in the cosmos according to which we inhabit an awkward middle space, affording us neither an understanding of the void from whence we came nor a meaningful grasp of the infinity that encloses us. "The end of things," writes Pascal, "and their beginning are insuperably hidden for [us] in an impenetrable secret" (67). Humanity knows neither where it comes from nor where it is going; and the result of our ignorance is terror. Houellebecq recalls his first brush as a teenager with Pascal, and with this terror, in a passage in *Public Enemies*:

> Pascal, if one takes into context the original violence of his writings, can produce a greater shock to the system than even the heaviest of heavy metal groups. The famous phrase "The eternal silence of these infinite spaces terrifies me" is too well known and has lost its impact, but it must be remembered that I was reading it for the first time [. . .] and I took it *full in the face*. The terror of infinite, empty space, into which one tumbles for all eternity [. . .]. After Pascal, all the suffering in the world was ready to surge into me. I

began to close my shutters on Sunday afternoon to listen to France Culture radio, [. . .] to buy records by the Velvet Underground and The Stooges, to read Nietzsche, Kafka, Dostoyevsky, and soon after, Balzac, Proust, all the rest. (Houellebecq and Lévy 2011, 135–37)

Houellebecq's early encounter with Pascal finds its most obvious expression in *The Elementary Particles*, for in this novel the concept of space—understood as "separation, distance, and suffering" (251)—constitutes the entire existential dilemma of an atomized human race grown weary of its existence. "Uneducated man," Djerzinski comments near the end of the novel, "is terrified by the idea of space; he imagines it to be vast, dark and yawning [. . .]. Terrified of the idea of space, human beings curl up; they feel cold, they feel afraid. At best, they move in space and greet one another sadly. And yet this space is within them, it is nothing but their mental creation" (251). Djerzinski is able to bring relief to humanity by undoing, if only in a metaphorical sense, the very intuition of space that, in the Kantian view, forms the basis of our perception. The race of clones that appears in *Particles*' closing pages has transcended the illusion of separation thanks to a few propitious changes to the human genetic code and, moreover, has adopted the worldview of an "ontology of states," based on an application of quantum mechanics to macrophysical systems, which replaces the "ontology of objects" that prevailed during our current "materialist age." The whole of *The Elementary Particles* can be read as an attempt to transcend the Pascalian conception of space—not only philosophically, as Kant did in the eighteenth century by identifying space as a "mere" psychological intuition, but concretely, through a reconstruction of the human genome according to a postmaterialist conception of the physical world.

Houellebecq's other novels can be read along similar lines: surely, something in the fear of separation and the loneliness afflicting characters such as Daniel1, Michel of *Platform*, and the narrator of *Whatever* can be traced to a more general existential horror of the void. In the last entry in his life story, Daniel1 writes,

> We are in September, the last vacationers are about to leave; with them the last breasts, the last bushes; the last accessible microworlds. An endless autumn awaits me, followed by a sidereal winter; and this time I really have finished my task, I am well past the very last minutes, there is no more justification for my presence

> here, no more human contact, no more assignable objective. There is, however, something else, something terrible, which floats in space, and seems to want to approach me. Before any sadness, any sorrow, or any clearly definable loss, there is something else, which might be called the *pure terror of space.* (296)

Space is the primordial terror, the first separation, and the last destiny. With no more "breasts" or "bushes" to connect him to humanity, Daniel1 is swallowed by the eternal silence of the infinite.

Here again, however, too strict a comparison of Houellebecq and his antecedent begins to encounter problems. Pascal was aware, and frightfully so, of humanity's clumsy station between the massive and the minuscule, of our galling ignorance of ultimate causes and ultimate ends. But he had a ready cure for his terror—his belief in God—and Houellebecq can boast no similarly and immediately effective remedy (so long as we grant that tampering with human genetics represents a cumbersome, paltry, and otherwise ethically fraught alternative). Houellebecq borrows all the terror of Pascal's cosmology but none of its solace, and to call Houellebecq Pascalian in any full sense would be like calling a person Christian who believes in the Fall but not in the redemption of the cross. Pascal has ready words to describe a person like Houellebecq. In pensée 681, which appears under the heading "A Letter to Further the Search for God," he writes: "I have nothing but pity for those who sincerely lament their doubting, who regard it as the ultimate misfortune, and who, sparing nothing to escape it, make of this search their most principal and most serious occupation" (1995, 159). Pascal has open contempt for those who brag of their indifference to the Ultimate, accusing such prideful doubters of "supernatural sloth" (162) and of being "deranged" (160); but for those who seek in spite of doubt, who doubt despite seeking, he has both respect and great sympathy: "there are only two sorts of people who can be called reasonable: those who serve God with all their heart because they know him, and those who seek him with all their heart because they do not know him" (163). Houellebecq is this second sort of person—if we extend Pascal's comment from its Christian context into a more universal seeking for salvation from the ways of the world. Houellebecq is a writer who, as Pascal puts it, sees in the news of the soul's extinction "something to say sadly, as the saddest thing in the world" (163), and for this reason he becomes worthy of Pascal's pity.

Like so many other students of the human condition (one might think of Tolstoy in his *Confession*, or even the Buddha), Houellebecq is concerned most primarily in his work with conveying the horror and tragedy of human life stripped of its metaphysical consolations. A full appreciation of Houellebecq's oeuvre requires a certain existential bravery, a willingness to grant that the world described by much of science and contemporary philosophy—a world without soul, without spirit, in which a human being is at best a happy biological accident—is a morally and existentially unacceptable world; that a civilization in which the human being, liberated from his or her traditional fetters, is paradoxically reduced to a unit of economic and sexual exchange is morally insufferable; and that, most contentiously of all, such a world, such a civilization, cannot hope to endure for long, but is prone to replacement by an order capable of better satisfying our existential needs. How long can the West—can any civilization—continue without God? This question lies at the heart of Houellebecq's fiction, and it receives its most definitive answer in what is Houellebecq's most provocative novel, *Submission*.

Liberalism Is God and the West Is Its Prophet

It's probably impossible for people who have lived and prospered in a given social system to imagine the point of view of those who, never having had anything to expect from that system, imagine its destruction without any particular alarm.

—Houellebecq 2015a (my translation)

The publication on January 7, 2015, of Houellebecq's sixth novel, *Submission*,[1] was part of one of the most bizarre and horrific coincidences in the history of contemporary literature. Houellebecq's face appeared on the cover of that morning's edition of *Charlie Hebdo*, a quintessentially haggard image of the author smoking a cigarette, and he declared that in 2022 he would participate in Ramadan; later that morning, Houellebecq lost his friend Bernard Maris, a contributor to *Charlie Hebdo* and the author of a 2014 book on Houellebecq, in the deadly attacks on the newspaper's office.

Houellebecq had written what seemed on all accounts to be an Islamophobic book—a paranoid tome recounting the horror of France's Islamicization after a Muslim is elected president in 2022, ahead of the National Front's Marine Le Pen. Houellebecq had already been taken to court and then acquitted on charges of inciting racial hatred against Muslims after claiming in an interview more than a dozen years ago that Islam was the "stupidest" religion. Certain of his novels' minor Muslim characters had denounced their religion in terms so categorical that Houellebecq, had *he* been Muslim, would have likely earned a fatwa similar to that pronounced on Salman Rushdie for his *Satanic Verses*. That *Submission* would continue in the same vein seemed the most logical thing in the world. French president François Hollande, interviewed a few days before the appearance of the novel, promised to read the book but warned that in literature there had always been "forces of regression" (Bonnefous 2015, n.p.), and he urged the French not to let themselves be "devoured by fear" (Vertaldi 2015, n.p.).

The coincidence of the attacks, the novel's publication, and *Charlie Hebdo*'s coverage of it thus spawned a tantalizing, unspoken suspicion: that the perceived Islamophobia of Houellebecq's latest effort had played a role, however figurative, in the massacre. Such a question appropriately took second place to the debates over religion and free speech that arose in the wake of the tragedy, as well as to national mourning. Indeed, no explicit statement, as far as I have been able to discover, was ever made connecting Houellebecq to the attackers' motives, the knowledge of which died with them. However, what did seem clear initially—and not only to the French president—was that Houellebecq's novel played into cultural paranoia about Islam, terrorism, and national and civilizational decline;[2] it would provide a symbol and a weapon for European nativist groups, such as Germany's Pegida, worried about the loss of national, racial, and religious identity; and it certainly did not affirm the kind of constructive discourse about tolerance and diversity that would, it seems, be likely to prevent a repetition of the *Charlie Hebdo* massacre in the future.

Submission quickly became a best seller throughout Europe, climbing to the top of the sales lists in France, Italy, and Germany (Hofmann 2015). But as critics began to digest the novel, it became apparent that Houellebecq's latest work could only very dubiously be judged Islamophobic in any strict sense. Strangely enough, the novel at places seems to *extol* Islam as the only possible cultural, religious, and economic replacement for a Europe, and specifically a France, that had long ago abandoned Christianity and now wallowed in an incoherent liberalism. *Submission*, as Adam Gopnik (2015) points out in the *New Yorker*, is not Islamophobic but rather is *Francophobic*. Like previous Houellebecqian works, the novel takes great pains to point out the disasters produced by the culture of "freedom" and "human rights" inherited from the Enlightenment: the decline of religion and the family, the anxiety of individualism, the confusion of gender roles, the proliferation of a sexual marketplace that replaces a culture in which adultery is prohibited, and so on. The novels *Whatever*, *The Elementary Particles*, and *The Possibility of an Island* had already dealt with these in detail; the difference in *Submission* is that the solution Houellebecq imagines to the woes of modernity is an extant faith tradition rather than an extraterrestrial religion or a cloning cult (see Houellebecq 2015b). Mark Lilla in the *New York Review of Books* offers perhaps the most enlightened summary of *Submission*'s target:

> Houellebecq's critics see the novel as anti-Muslim because they assume that individual freedom is the highest human value—and have convinced themselves that the Islamic tradition agrees with them. It does not, and neither does Houellebecq. Islam is not the target of *Soumission* [. . .]. It serves as a device to express a very persistent European worry that the single-minded pursuit of freedom—freedom from tradition and authority, freedom to pursue one's own ends—must inevitably lead to disaster. (2015, n.p.)

Submission is a continuation of Houellebecq's unflagging attack on liberalism and the boasts of freedom in all forms. In this case, however, the warning is all the more urgent and apparent: different from the utopian phantasms that Houellebecq imagines in previous novels, Islam represents, at least in some of its iterations, a real and tempting solution to Westerners who have lost their spiritual way. That *Submission* paints Islam in the most flattering possible light thus stands as a kind of challenge to Houellebecq's readers. It is as if the novel asks, "Read and tell me if you do not, somewhere in your heart, feel tempted by this vision of a Europe in which family life has been restored, men and women have their assigned roles, the economy has been stabilized, and eternal life is reaffirmed." Like Houellebecq's other novels, *Submission* wonders whether the anxieties of modernity and of individual freedom are worth the benefits they (allegedly) produce. This is a question that the modern West has always faced in one form or another, and it is through the prism of Islam that it asks the question today.

The Modern Western Woman: A Two-Hundred-Year Disaster in the Making

Of all the social groups in Houellebecq's novels that have suffered the anxieties of freedom, women stand out as a particularly egregious example of liberation gone over to the dark side. One of the advantages of *Submission* is that its engagement with a living religion allows it to draw a sharp contrast between liberated women and traditional women—that is, between modern Western women and women living "in submission," that is, under Islam.

François, the novel's forty-four-year-old protagonist and narrator, describes the erotic life of an ex-girlfriend named Aurélie, with whom he briefly (and unromantically) reunites early in the novel: "As for the present, it was obvious that Aurélie had in no way managed to embark upon a conjugal relationship, that her occasional adventures caused her a growing sense of disgust, and that, to sum it up, her sentimental life was heading toward total and irremediable disaster" (2015a, 21). Another former girlfriend, Sandra, who according to François "leaves a less profound impression of dereliction" (22), is nonetheless prey to a "not perfectly extinguished sensuality" (24) that "would push her to seek the company of young people," in turn leading her to become what François "in his youth" referred to as a "cougar" (24). Even so, the best Sandra can hope for is perhaps a dozen years of erotic adventure before the "crippling decline of her flesh led her to permanent solitude" (24). The notion that either of these women, after experiencing "ten or twenty" "amorous relationships of variable duration," should "as a pinnacle of achievement" get married and have children strikes François as perfectly inane (21). Where Aurélie is irreparably bitter after the failure of a relationship (21), the description of Sandra's cougarish predilections takes on a most pathetic quality in the mind of the reader. Left to their choices to pursue sexual freedom, to multiply their erotic adventures, while at the same time devoting their days to a demanding career—in other words, goaded on by women's liberation to imitate the customs of men—these women have met with sentimental and sensual disasters. In a society that insisted that women marry early and raise children and that severely punished infidelity, such catastrophes would be avoided; this, at any rate, is François's implicit conclusion.

This is not to say that François is any kind of engaged chauvinist. A depressive, lonely, alcoholic university professor who only dates his former students, François describes himself to his sometimes girlfriend, Myriam, as a "sort [of] vague chauvinist" who has "never been persuaded that it's a good idea that women should be able to vote, take the same classes as men, or have access to the same professions" (41) but who has no will to stand in the way of women's "progress." "I'm not *for* anything at all," he tells Myriam during an evening together in his apartment, "but patriarchy at least had the merit of existing, that is to say as a social system it persevered. [. . .] there were families with children, who more or less produced the same pattern" (41). Myriam's patience is extreme in dealing with François, though she protests: "Let's say that you're right about patriarchy, that it's the only viable option. All the same, I've studied, gotten used to thinking of myself as an individual person, endowed with a capacity for thinking and decision making equal to that of men, so what's to be done with me, then? Am I good for nothing?" (43). Wanting to spare Myriam's feelings, François says only to himself, "The right answer was probably 'Yes'" (44). Myriam is in her early twenties and has the whole of her life in front of her; it will be many years before she begins to experience the disappointment, bitterness, and, of course, physical decline of Aurélie and Sandra. In many ways, female bodies serve as a kind of proxy for Houellebecq's rendering of modern French history. Just as the youthful Myriam is able to enjoy all the pleasures of liberation while Aurélie and Sandra must suffer all its deceits, so the early revolutionary society of Robespierre, Fourier, and Comte could revel in the emancipation from tradition, while the France of François's time is left in postmodern dereliction.

Submission's most striking example of modern female affliction comes in the person of Annelise, the wife of Bruno,[3] François's fellow graduate student who leaves academia to become a tax inspector after defending his dissertation. Annelise works long hours as a marketing executive for a mobile telephone company. It is worth quoting François's description of her in its entirety:

> I thought about Annelise's life, and about that of all western women. In the morning she probably did her hair and then dressed carefully, as her professional status called for, and I think that in her case she was more elegant than sexy [. . .]. She must have spent a lot of time on it before taking the children to day care, then the day was spent dealing with emails, on the telephone, and in various meetings. When she returned home exhausted around nine o'clock, she would collapse, put on a sweatshirt and sweatpants, and this was how she presented herself to her lord and master, and he must have had, he must necessarily have had the feeling of having gotten screwed somewhere, and she herself had the feeling of having gotten screwed somewhere, and that the passing of years would bring no resolution, nor would the children's growing up or

the mechanical increase in professional responsibilities, and this without even taking into account the drooping of the flesh. (93–94)

Annelise is the cliché of the modern superwoman, balancing work, children, and a marriage; in other words, she is totally miserable. But she is not the only one. Bruno, no doubt forced to share domestic duties with his wife while pursuing his career, is equally conscious of "having gotten screwed" somewhere. Women's liberation and marriage are incompatible; the blurring of gender roles leads only to confusion and exhaustion; and the incoherent family life that results is a source of anxiety and disappointment.

These criticisms of modern marriage are in no way new. A brief survey of literature on the "end of men" reveals a growing complaint on the part of both men and women in the West that unhinged feminism has emasculated men and transformed marriage from a partnership with well-defined roles to a zero-sum game in which husband and wife compete for dominance.[4] *Submission* plays cleverly and provocatively on these issues, but the novel's true contribution to the debate lies in how Houellebecq is able to contrast the disorder plaguing gender relations in the contemporary West with the harmonization of male and female roles that an Islamic society promises. Unsurprisingly, Houellebecq's first target is the female body. On the one hand, Western women like Annelise are obliged by their social status to be "classy and sensual during the day," but upon returning home they "exhaustedly [renounce] any possibility of seduction, throwing on loose and formless clothing" (91). Muslim women, on the other hand, compelled by their religion to don "impenetrable black burkas during the day" (91), nonetheless metamorphose in the evening into "birds of paradise, adorning themselves in corsets, openwork bras, thongs decorated with colorful lace and precious stones" (91). They are, in other words, the "exact opposite of western women" (91). While strolling through the Place d'Italie, François predicts (and later his prediction is confirmed) that stores catering to Western women's sartorial tastes, such as Jennyfer, will disappear under an Islamic regime, while Secret Stories, a boutique selling off-label lingerie, will flourish (90–91). The only effect he notes in the wake of sexuality's flight from public space once the Muslim Brotherhood comes to power is that "the contemplation of women's buttocks, a minimal, dreamy consolation, had also become impossible" (177).

Women's economic autonomy also comes in for stern critique in *Submission*. Having taken firm control of the French educational system, the newly elected president, Mohammed Ben Abbes, and his administration quickly establish policies that point women in the direction of homemaking schools once they have completed their primary education and that encourage them to marry as quickly as possible (82). Only a small minority, as François's acquaintance Alain Tanneur, a former member of the French intelligence service, explains, will be allowed to "study art or literature before marrying" (82). The immediate consequence of women's departure from the economic sphere and return to homemaking is a drastic reduction in the rate of men's unemployment—that is, an end to one of the principal economic afflictions of modern France and much of the rest of Western Europe (199). *Submission* makes no attempt to paint these changes in women's autonomy in a negative light. In fact, it is the very notion of autonomy as a key Western value that the novel calls into question. While riding a train back to Paris, François notes the giddy, innocent happiness of two adolescent girls, who are married to a visibly anxious and overworked Arab businessman:

> In an Islamic regime, women—well, those who were pretty enough to arouse the desire of a wealthy husband—had [. . .] the possibility of remaining children practically their whole lives. Shortly after the end of childhood, they themselves became mothers and were again immersed in a child's universe. Their children grew up, then they became grandmothers, and their lives went on in this way. There were only a few years where they bought sexy underwear, trading children's games for sexual ones—which amounted to about the same thing. Obviously they lost their autonomy, but *fuck autonomy*.[5] (227)

François, removed from his university position after refusing to convert to Islam, is "obliged to agree" that he has "easily renounced, and even with true relief" any sort of professional or intellectual responsibility, and he in no way envies the life of the Arab businessman whose face becomes "almost gray with anguish" (227) as he speaks on the telephone with a colleague. "At least," François observes as he watches the threesome from the other side of the train car, "he would have the compensation of two gracious and charming wives to distract him from the concerns of an exhausted businessman" (227). Women's return to puerility under the Muslim Brotherhood is a boon for both sexes: women are relieved of the burden of individualism and self-determination, while men have the comfort of companions who in no way remind the men of their professional responsibilities, but rather permit them to escape, if only for a short time, into a world of innocent sexuality and domestic harmony where they can lay down the burden of their labors. *Submission* is not a chauvinistic fantasy about male control of female sexuality. If anything, it is women, having suffered more than men from the anxieties of freedom, who benefit most under the new regime, while men are still compelled to live the larger portion of their lives within the domain of economic struggle.

At its most essential, *Submission* is a rebuke of two forms of liberalism that Houellebecq has consistently portrayed as inimical to human happiness: the first, sexual liberalism, has ruined marriage and compromised the basic unit of social life, the family; and the second, epistemological liberalism, frees man from divine command and thus subjects the "truth" to competition and the corroding and secularizing forces of relativism. *Submission*'s Muslim Brotherhood, while leaving economic freedom untouched (153), recognizes the mischief that these other two forms of liberation have wrought in the West—and the group responds accordingly. And it is François, embodying the anxiety of these freedoms, though acutely incapable of reaction against them, who represents at once the Islamic regime's foil and its raison d'être.

As Goes France, So Goes François

Submission is in large part a conversion narrative, though of a sort manifestly different from those told by the French intellectual converts of a century or more past (see chapter 3). Houellebecq had originally intended to title his novel *La Conversion* rather than *Soumission*, with the main character converting to Catholicism by the book's end. The goal, as he explains in the *Paris Review*, was to have his protagonist follow in the footsteps of fellow novelist Joris-Karl Huysmans, who abandoned naturalism for the Catholic Church late in his career. Much of this interest in conversion is due to Houellebecq's newfound ambivalence toward atheism, which, he confesses, "hasn't quite survived all the deaths I've had to deal with." He explains, "Part of it may be that, contrary to what I thought, I never was quite an atheist. I was an agnostic. Usually that word serves as a screen for atheism but not, I think, in my case. When, in the light of what I know, I reexamine the question whether there is a creator, a cosmic order, that kind of thing, I realize that I don't actually have an answer" (2015b, n.p.).

François's conversion in *Submission* is not, however, to Catholicism or any kind of Christianity. An internationally respected scholar of Huysmans—François has written a dissertation and a book on the author and is tapped later in the novel to edit a Pléiade edition of Huysmans's collected works—François's attempts to allay his prototypically Houellebecquian malaise will fall short of the successes of his intellectual hero (who, as François and Houellebecq rightly note, converted to Catholicism for largely aesthetic reasons).[6] Rather, and much more topically, François's vector in *Submission* is toward an ascendant Islam. As becomes clear to François later on, Islam and Christianity, whatever their apparent differences, are both interested in the same thing, namely, an escape from the atheistic humanism that has dominated France and the West since the beginning of the revolutionary period. The Christian dispensation was at its apogee in the Middle Ages; its time has come and gone, and, as Houellebecq has insisted throughout his career whenever accused of being a reactionary, there can be no going back to a previous time. Huysmans's choice subsequent to *À rebours* may have been between a crucifix and the business end of a pistol;[7] for François, the decision will be between suicide and the Islamic crescent.

With the exception of his academic achievements, François is a characteristic Houellebecquian loser: an amalgam of loneliness, depression, alcoholism, neurotic introversion, and misanthropy that, among other things, makes him an appropriate subject for satirizing contemporary academic life. Renowned in France for his work on Huysmans, François places little stock in his professional success, going so far as to insinuate that his "clear, decisive," and "brilliant" articles are "generally respected" because he is "never late on deadlines" (47). François has little interest in his students; having arranged to teach all his classes on a single day of the week (27), he complains of "nasty" graduate students who pester him with "idle questions" about minor French poets (53–54). His love life is a series of erotic encounters with female students, none of them lasting more than a year, which, as the years pass, take on a "dimension of transgression" linked more to the "development of his university status" than his "real or even apparent aging" (23). Considering his scholarly accomplishments, François wonders, "was this enough to justify a life[?]" (47). At forty-four, his best years, both professionally and personally, seem to be behind him. "What would I become at age fifty, sixty, or more?" he asks himself. "By then I'd only be a slowly decomposing hodgepodge of organs, and my life would become an endless torture, grim, nasty, and without joy" (99). Having lost interest in his career and nearing an age where he can no longer count on the affections of his students, François charts a path not unlike Daniel of *The Possibility of an Island* or Bruno of *The Elementary Particles.* His only solace is his love for Huysmans, whom he rereads somewhat obsessively while alone in his apartment, all the while imbibing (and this is no surprise) large quantities of wine.

François's malaise is set against the backdrop of a political drama—the rise of the Muslim Brotherhood in France—that will fundamentally alter the country's political and social life. At the head of these developments is Mohammed Ben Abbes, the party's candidate in the 2022 presidential race, who, after ousting the socialists in the first round of the election, goes on to defeat Marine Le Pen in a runoff to become France's first Muslim president. Abbes has little interest in economic reform; indeed, the country's fiscal woes are largely remedied by an influx of money from the Gulf petromonarchies, which appear willing to contribute any amount of money to swell the prosperity of their first true ally in the West. Rather, Ben Abbes's concerns are social and, of course, religious in nature:

> Ben Abbes had [. . .] avoided compromising himself with the anti-capitalist left; the liberal right had won the "battle of ideas," he had understood this perfectly, young people had become *entrepreneurial*, and the inimitable character of the market economy was at present unanimously accepted. But above all, the true stroke of genius of the Muslim leader had been to understand that elections would not play out on the economic field, but rather on that of values. (153)

"Perfectly sincere when he proclaims his respect for the three religions of the Book," Ben Abbes's true objective in the domain of social values is not Islam's supplanting of an already hobbled Catholicism, but rather the destabilization and dismantling of the cult of "secularism, *laïcité*," and "atheist materialism" that, in the party's view, goes further toward explaining the decline of European civilization than any economic considerations ever could (156). Modern Europeans are hungry for the return of religion, and education, as Ben Abbes and his party recognize early on, will be the key site for the revival of a neglected Western soul:

> More and more often, families—be they Jewish, Christian, or Muslim—would want schooling for their children that wasn't limited

> to the transmission of knowledge, but that included spiritual education corresponding to their tradition. This return of the religious was a deep trend, and the national education system couldn't not take it into account. All in all, it was a matter of broadening the scope of republican education, of making it capable of harmonious coexistence alongside the great spiritual traditions—Muslim, Christian, or Jewish—of our country. (108–9)

As an accomplished academic, François stands directly in the path of the pedagogical bulldozer that the Muslim Brotherhood intends to drive over Parisian university culture.[8] Once the party takes control of education, professors are given the choice of conversion to Islam or retirement with a handsome pension. Unsurprisingly, François chooses the latter option, but he is astounded to find that his colleagues who have agreed to stay on under the new terms (i.e., conversion) are paid a salary three times higher than the previous prevailing wage, are housed in elegant apartments on the Boulevard Saint-Germain, and, most important, are promised wives from among their students.

Like all of Houellebecq's protagonists, François is a religious anemic. The idea that he might become a believer of any sort strikes him not so much as undesirable but as simply impossible. Not until the election of Ben Abbes does he give any serious consideration to religious matters: "For the first time in my life I had begun thinking about God, seriously envisioning the idea of a Creator of the Universe, who watched over each of my acts, and my first reaction was very definite: it was none other than fear" (263). The only religious sensibility he betrays is embedded in his love for Huysmans, who at age forty-four converted to Catholicism at a monastery in the Marne. François, in many ways a kind of secular monastic, seems to yearn for the piety and simplicity of monastery life: "In a monastery, one escaped the greater part of [life's] concerns; one laid down the burden of individual existence" (99). "In a monastery," he continues, "you're assured food and shelter—along with, as a bonus, eternal life in the best of cases" (100). As France is roiled by political and social disorder not seen since the world wars, François, having fled Paris for southwestern France, visits the Black Madonna of Rocamadour, hoping the visit will inspire in him something of the pious sentiment that led Huysmans to the foot of the crucifix more than a century ago.

The effort will, of course, be a failure. François's initial impression of the imposing black virgin is a mixture of anachronism and holy terror:

> It was a strange statue, bearing witness to an altogether forgotten age. The Virgin was sitting very straight; her face, its eyes closed, so distant as to seem unearthly, was crowned by a diadem. The baby Jesus [. . .] was also sitting very straight on her knees; his eyes were also closed, and his sharp, wise, powerful face was surmounted by a crown as well. There was no tenderness, no maternal abandon in their attitudes. It was not the baby Jesus who was represented; he was, already, the king of the world. His serenity, the impression of spiritual power, of intangible might that he emitted was almost frightening. (166)

This is not the friendly Jesus of contemporary catechism. Here is the representation of a true king of kings, presiding over a medieval Christendom that endured for more than a millennium, compared to which the revolutionary society that Europe spawned after the Enlightenment appears as little more than a brief interim between millennial spiritual dispensations (162). As François contemplates the virgin, he feels a growing desire to lose himself, to abandon his ego and individuality to an ancient spiritual power, to be relieved of the autonomy and struggle of the modern Westerner—to submit, as it were, to this erstwhile lord of the Western world (169). The experience, however, is fleeting; François even wonders whether his apparent brush with the mystical may not have been a result of having forgotten to eat the night before at the hotel (169). The next morning, before leaving by car to return to Paris, François goes to see the statue a second time: "She possessed dominion, she possessed power, but little by little I felt I was losing contact, that she was drifting away, disappearing into the centuries, while I slumped in my pew [. . .]. At the end of fifteen minutes I got up, permanently abandoned by the Spirit, reduced to my run-down, perishable body, and I sadly descended the steps in the direction of the parking lot" (170).

A return to the bosom of Europe's native Christianity is not an option for François, any more than it is for France. Christendom, he realizes as the virgin fades into the mists of the past, no longer speaks to modern man; its power to command and to sanctify belongs to a forgotten age, and there can be no going back. It is an exceedingly sad vision: a spiritual order that organized human life for more than ten centuries, but that is no more able to save itself from the destructive forces of rationalism than was the Roman Empire able to save itself from collapse at the end of the fifth century (276).[9]

Back in Paris and without work, François dreads the empty existence that he will now be obliged to traverse: "I felt nothing more than a muted, deadened pain. [. . .] all that I saw was that once again I was alone, with a desire to live that was dwindling, with numerous worries to look forward to" (196). François is a kind of carcass of revolutionary civilization. Everything that freedom from tradition, from God, and from the church promised has become for him a source of despair and meaninglessness, just as it has for his contemporaries. He is an embodiment of every anxiety of which one could reasonably accuse modernity, including atheism, meaninglessness, sexual immorality, and dereliction of parenthood; and it is precisely this spiritual and moral indisposition that Abbes and his party seek to treat. Knowing that he will die "rapidly, miserable and alone" (249) in his present state, Islam thus begins to loom large for François.

A Conversion *au conditionnel*

On his return to Paris, François is surprised to discover a letter in his mailbox from Bastien Lacoue, the chief editor at Éditions de la Pléiade,[10] proposing that François edit the complete works of Joris-Karl Huysmans. Instantly aware that "this was not the kind of proposition one refuses" (229), François, treating himself to a heavy dose of Calvados to calm his nerves, takes a meeting with Lacoue two days later at the publisher's Gallimard offices. Lacoue, who during the meeting somewhat cheekily opines that the Bibliothèque de la Pléiade is in the business of working "for eternity" (231), quickly convinces François to accept his offer. More important, Lacoue persuades François to attend a reception in honor of the reopening of the Sorbonne (that is, the Université Islamique Paris–Sorbonne, now largely funded by Saudi oil dollars) in order to meet the university's new president, Robert Rediger, who, François senses from Lacoue's remarks, is eager to lure François back into the ranks of the Parisian intellectual elite.

Rediger is a mixture of physical superman and expert proselytizer: tall, powerfully built, dressed in jeans and a leather jacket (238), his casual virility seems out of sync with his role as an intellectual leader (especially a French intellectual leader). His manners, and especially his smile, are nonetheless irresistible. At the conclusion of the reception—attended exclusively by men, many of whom are members of the delegation of a Saudi prince who has come to meet the minister of national education—Rediger, consciously brandishing his disarming smile, asks François to meet with him privately at his home several days later. François, somewhat star struck, agrees immediately.

Luxuriously housed near the Arènes de Lutèce and recently married to a fifteen-year-old girl name Aïcha, Rediger offers what is surely the firmest repudiation of European modernity and Enlightenment civilization that Houellebecq has ever mustered in fiction. As he treats François to "an excellent Meursault" (244) in his vast library-salon, Rediger expounds at length on the personal journey that led him to Islam: his early discovery of the moral and spiritual emptiness of atheistic humanism, a youthful romance with Christian identity movements (*mouvements identitaires*), and finally a painful realization, much like François's malaise before the Black Madonna of Rocamadour, that Christianity had no hope of revitalizing the soul of Western civilization, that its time had passed, and that Islam occupied the ascendant in the West's spiritual future. "Without Christianity," Rediger tells François, "the European nations were no more than bodies without souls—zombies" (255). He continues a couple of pages later:

> This Europe that was the summit of human civilization has well and truly committed suicide, in the space of several decades [. . .]. There were throughout Europe anarchist and nihilist movements, calls to violence, the negation of all moral law. And then, a few years later, everything ended in that inexcusable madness of the First World War [. . .]. If France and Germany, the two most advanced, civilized nations could abandon themselves to this senseless butchery, then that was because Europe was dead. (257)

Having grasped some ten years ago the extent of the destruction, both spiritual and material, that atheistic humanism—that is, the collapse of Christianity—had wrought in the West, the next day Rediger went to visit an imam in Brussels and "in the presence of about ten witnesses [. . .] utter[ed] the ritual formula of conversion to Islam" (257).

François, however, has an objection: is it really true, he asks, that contemporary Europeans are as hungry for God and religious revival as Rediger suggests? "I had the impression," he tells Robert, "[. . .] that atheism was universally spread throughout the western world" (250), in other words that its foundation in the West is solid and that Islam poses no real threat as a "Great Replacement," especially in the presence of an improving economy. Rediger sweeps François's concerns aside: "It is for metaphysical questions that men fight, certainly not for an uptick in economic growth or for the division of hunting territory [. . .]. Even in the West, in reality, atheism has no solid base" (251). He continues, borrowing from the theory of intelligent design:

> The Universe evidently bears the mark of intelligent design. [. . .] it is obviously the realization of a project conceived by an immense intelligence. And sooner or later this idea was going to impose itself again, that was something I had understood when I was very young. The whole intellectual debate of the twentieth century had come down to an opposition between communism—let's call it the *hard* version of humanism—and liberal democracy—its soft version; this was nonetheless terribly reductive. (253–54)

Rediger's attempt at proselytism (a digest version of Frankfurt School philosophy with Voltaire's watchmaker argument thrown into the mix) fails to convince François in its immediate aftermath. Even so, having returned home with a copy of Robert's *Ten Questions About Islam* under his arm, François spends an anxious night worrying that an angry God might be waiting to punish him for his sins—perhaps by smiting him with a cancer of the jaw much like that which afflicted Huysmans (263–64). The next morning, returning to Rediger's *maison particulière* to pick up the backpack he left the night before, François walks through the Latin Quarter, stopping in front of the Grand Mosque of Paris and making a few general observations about the ugliness of contemporary architecture, before going home to read Rediger's book.

Apart from some extended remarks on European history and spiritual decadence (which he finds rather dubious in their simplicity), François is most struck in his reading of *Ten Questions About Islam* by Rediger's treatment of polygamy and the role of the "dominant male" in propagating the human species: "The inequality between males—if certain of them saw themselves accorded the pleasure of several females, others would necessarily have to be deprived—was [. . .] not supposed to be considered a perverse effect of polygamy, but well and truly its real objective. It was in this way that the species accomplished its destiny" (260). François naturally fears he will be among those left to suffer the "perverse effect" of polygamy. More akin to the narrator of *Whatever* than he is to the virile Robert, he suspects that a conversion to Islam will leave him no less lonely than he is at present.

François quickly finishes the introduction to his Pléiade edition, noting that his "very long relationship with Joris-Karl Huysmans" (283) has come to an end, and takes his concerns about polygamy to Rediger, who is more than pleased to put François's mind at ease on this delicate point: "Man is an animal, that's clear; but he's neither a prairie dog nor an antelope. It's neither his claws, nor his teeth, nor how fast he runs that assures him a dominant place in nature; but rather his intelligence. So I'm telling you this very seriously: there's nothing abnormal in the idea that university professors should be counted among the dominant males" (292). After a few encouraging comments from Rediger on the advantages of arranged marriage, François seems persuaded.[11] Acknowledging that his professional career is over (or that he can now rest on his laurels while attending "vague colloquia"; 295) and desperately afraid of loneliness in old age, he suddenly has the sensation, extraordinary for a Houellebecquian protagonist, that "there would be [. . .] something else" (295) to live for.

And so François converts. Or, at the very least, the reader encounters a kind of hypothetical conversion scenario in which all the action is conveyed not in the narrative past but rather in the conditional tense (which I have indicated in italics):

> Images of constellations, supernovas, and nebulas *would cross* my mind; images of springs as well, of inviolate mineral deserts, of great, nearly virgin forests; little by little, I *would be penetrated* by the grandeur of the cosmic order. Then, in a calm voice, I *would utter* the following formula [. . . :] "I testify that there is no other God than God, and that Mohammed is his prophet." And then it *would be* over; I *would be*, from then on, a Muslim. (298)

What is the meaning of this seemingly conditional conversion? Is it intended simply to convey a kind of mystical dreaminess—the happy expectations of a man who has been won over to Allah and contemplates with eager anticipation a new and happier life? Or is Houellebecq instead leaving the question of whether François converts in doubt, in a kind of hypothetical or liminal suspension? And if so, why?

Reaction, Romanticism, or Something Else?

Before attempting an answer to the question in the heading, I consider, and in some respects anticipate, two possible—indeed, probable—readings of

Houellebecq's *Submission*. The first is that this novel is a reactionary text championing as much the renewal of European Christianity as the evisceration of Islam's influence in the West. The second potential reading is that such championing represents not so much a reaction against Islam but a kind of romantic evocation of a lost era of medieval existential unity. The second reading is somewhat more plausible than the first, but both strike me as insufficient to give a full account of the novel. Ultimately, *Submission* is posing a question to Europe, and particularly to France, about its own soul, an interrogation of the limits and costs of revolution and unfettered liberalism in the context of a growing imperialistic Islam, which each reader is called upon to answer according to his or her own conscience. The novel is the most powerful sort of provocation, intended not to agitate readers out of some kind of authorial perversity but rather to push them toward what is perhaps the overwhelming question of late European modernity: how much longer can the current dispensation endure? How much longer can the ubiquitous ethos of multiculturalism, tolerance, inclusion, and secularism persist? And, most important, should they?

The charge of being reactionary has plagued Houellebecq from the beginning of his career, with both scholars and critics accusing the author of calling for a return to "traditional values" in an effort to staunch the bleeding provoked by excessive liberalism (e.g., Lindenberg 2002; van Wesemael 2005). *Submission* seems easily susceptible to such accusations, for the novel goes to great lengths to lament the moral degradation of Westerners, and specifically of Western women, in the absence of tradition, and moreover it explicitly suggests that an Islamic society would put a quick end to such turpitude. However, to interpret *Submission*'s treatment of women, for example, as reactionary in anything but the most general sense would be a mistake. The Islamic regime of polygamy, for example, is largely alien to the West; its inauguration as a popular cultural practice would constitute something quite *new*, as would the novel's standards for women's dress and education, as well as expectations for religious practice. In "returning" to traditional gender roles writ large, the West would certainly not be returning to its own premodern Christian (or prefeminist) past, but rather would be assuming the values of a competing civilization whose affinities with the West's heritage, if not incidental, are at least the product of very different historical developments. Indeed, characters such as Rediger, who imagine a revitalization of Christianity as a socially-structuring institution, are quickly overcome by a sense of futility. For example, Robert explains in *Ten Questions About Islam*:

> The Catholic Church had become incapable of opposing moral decadence, of clearly rejecting, and with vigor, homosexual marriage, abortion rights and women's labor. The truth was indisputable: having reached a degree of repugnant decomposition, western Europe was no longer capable of saving itself on its own—no more than was ancient Rome in the fifth century of our era [. . .]. Medieval Christianity had been a great civilization, whose artistic accomplishments would live eternally in human memory; but little by little it had lost ground, it had had to come to terms with rationalism, renounce the subjugation of temporal power, as such it had gradually condemned itself, and why? All things considered, it was a mystery; God had made it so. (276)

Islam represents a spiritual order able to dispel the moral darkness that the brief interim of revolutionary civilization has spread across the West and much of the rest of the globe. In an echo of Comtean positivism, Islam is called on to "create a new organic phase of civilization" founded on "the rejection of atheism and humanism, on the necessary submission of women, on the return of patriarchy" (275). This is not a reaction but rather a return to normal; the true reactionary player has all along been Enlightenment culture, which insists on an unsustainable assortment of freedoms largely inimical to human happiness. Islam stands for bringing humanity back to its senses. To call *Submission* reactionary would thus be to assume that liberal civilization and atheistic humanism represent the most natural state of human social organization and that a return to a more religious order constitutes a kind of primitivism—a rather dubious historical conjecture. This is not an assumption Islam shares, and neither does Houellebecq.

Nor is *Submission* a romantic elegy sung for a post-Christian Europe whose best days and most noble accomplishments seem to have faded, much like the Black Madonna of Rocamadour, into a vague and distant past. Houellebecq is, admittedly, indulging in a kind of romanticism in his evocation of a lost age of medieval piety—a tactic that results, as I showed in chapter 1, in a wholesale embrace of secularization theory and in the "horror" of a society utterly bereft of metaphysical consolations. For example, as

Tanneur explains to François early in the novel, "The French Revolution, the Republic, the fatherland . . . yes, that was able to give birth to something; something that lasted a little more than a century. Medieval Christianity, however, lasted more than a millennium" (162). Tanneur's implication is that a civilization grounded in divine sanction will endure far longer than a civilization without such a foundation. Revolutionary culture was a brief and somewhat curious experiment in human self-determination, and the disasters of the twentieth century offer clear evidence that the experiment was a failure. This is not romanticism but, at least as far as Houellebecq is concerned, a historical and sociological platitude. Whatever view one may hold about the putative universal piousness of the Christian Middle Ages, Houellebecq's intention, elaborated through his engagement with Comte, is not to romanticize a forsaken past but rather to insist on the irreducible necessity of a religiously grounded social order. *Submission* cannot be romantic for the same reason that it cannot be reactionary, because both interpretations of the novel would impute to Houellebecq an entertainment of the possibility of resurrecting a lost era of human harmony—a possibility that Houellebecq has consistently denied.

The key to understanding *Submission* lies instead in François's conditional conversion at the close of the novel. Houellebecq could have justifiably, and without any violation of the text's formal unity, chosen to situate the conversion scene in the narrative past. François's arc in the novel is unmistakable in its push toward some sort of conversion; indeed, that *Submission*'s conclusion is rendered as a hypothesis could reasonably strike attentive readers as something akin to an anticlimax. How to account for this narrative evasiveness, if evasiveness it truly is? The answer is that Houellebecq has left the matter of François's conversion up to his reader, and the reader will elect to render the ending in the narrative past depending on how successfully Houellebecq has seduced him or her with a kind of fatalism.

Houellebecq has spent the entirety of his career highlighting the moral and existential inadequacies of Enlightenment culture, most specifically in its liberal instantiation. The only real difference, the only real evolution, in *Submission* is that the solution to these inadequacies—Islam—is readily available to those who want it. Any reader, Western or otherwise, who has assumed as a mantle the Houellebecquian critique of liberalism cannot help but *want* François to convert to Islam—not, to be sure, the medieval Islam of the Islamic State or even the Islam of much of the Muslim world, but rather the gentle, moderate Islam of the Muslim Brotherhood, which soothes the spiritual wounds of modernity while avoiding the temptations of poisonous radicalism. *Submission* implicates the reader in its own finale, even as it embeds that finale in the resolution of many of France's major social and economic ills (rampant unemployment, economic stagnation, etc.). The French language even stands to gain as a consequence of Islam's ascendancy in France. Rediger explains: "Like Richelieu, Ben Abbes is getting ready to do an immense service to the French language. With the membership of the Arab countries, the European linguistic balance is going to swing in favor of France. Sooner or later, you'll see, there will be a proposed directive imposing French, on an equal footing with English, as the working language of European institutions" (291).

What can the erstwhile secular regime hope to offer in place of such an auspicious development? An endless concatenation of worsening debt crises? The slow and painful dissolution of the European Union and the renewal of all the old European rivalries? A return to the premodern Christian dispensation will not be possible, and modern Europe is doomed both spiritually and economically, and in short order. To label *Submission* as Islamophobic—that is, as anything other than Houellebecq's latest and perhaps most provocative attack on liberal Enlightenment culture—is to give evidence of not having read the novel at all. Rather, *Submission* challenges thoughtful readers to elaborate a wholly new response to the West's inadequacies, based neither in the Enlightenment and its most historically significant ideological offspring (socialism and liberalism) nor in the world's enduring religions, but rather in the invention of some totally new and as yet unheard-of economic, political, and metaphysical synthesis. The West seems today to be in desperate need of this, but, in an echo of Houellebecq's impotent protagonists, it appears sadly incapable of producing it.

In his review of *Submission* in the *New Yorker*, Adam Gopnik (2015) suggests that the evils plaguing France in Houellebecq's novel could be remedied by a few years of economic growth. If I have accomplished anything in this book, I hope to have persuaded the reader that this sort of economic reductionism is incapable of confronting the metaphysical anxieties that haunt modernity in Houellebecq's fiction. Perhaps more than any other modern Western country, France since the revolution has been afflicted by the anguish of its own precipitous departure from tradition, giving rise to an antimodern literary and philosophical canon that began with the likes of Maistre and Baudelaire (see Compagnon 2005), passed through the Catholic revivalist writers of the end of the nineteenth century and early twentieth, and finds its latest instantiation in Michel Houellebecq. The anxieties of freedom are not quelled by an uptick in economic growth; this is as obvious to the anti-immigrant factions gathering steam in Europe as it is to the radicalized Islamic movements to which they are a reaction. The modern West is today mired in the squalor of an exhausted prosperity; Houellebecq has understood this and explored its inevitable result. Only time will tell if the novelist attains the status of a prophet.

NOTES

Introduction

1. Writes Sweeney, "His novels can be read, on the one hand, as a reactionary response to the progressive socio-cultural movements of the twentieth century such as feminism and multiculturalism while on the other, they seem to offer a compelling critique of the totalizing mechanism of the 'market' with its hitherto unparalleled influence on human life" (2013, x). See Viard 2008, 38, for a similar analysis.

2. The two citations of Bellanger that follow are also my translations.

3. In other words, he blames himself.

4. Les Éditions de Minuit is a French publishing house famous for publishing the works of the *nouveau roman* authors, whose writing tends to be highly formalized.

5. I also do not want to imply that Houellebecq lacks style, as was somewhat inanely claimed by critics of his earlier novels. See Noguez 2003 for a discussion of Houellebecq's stylistic distinctiveness.

6. In the novella *Lanzarote*, the Belgian Rudi's marriage is destroyed after he and his wife spend several months going to swingers clubs in Brussels (2000b, 62–63).

7. The term "materialist horror" is suggested by Houellebecq in his epistolary exchange with Lévy. He writes, "Maybe, like Lovecraft, all I have ever written are *materialist horror stories* [*contes matérialistes d'épouvante* in the original French]; and given them a dangerous credibility into the bargain" (2011, 275).

8. I note here that I am using the term "religion" in a colloquial or perhaps traditionally Christian sense, referring to belief in God or gods, the soul and the afterlife, and the supernatural. From a scholarly point of view, the definition of "religion" is, of course, quite a bit more complicated; I take up this issue in my second chapter. Houellebecq, however, also understands "religion" in the more informal way, so it seems appropriate to engage him on his own terms.

9. For a detailed discussion of this sect, whose practices largely resemble those of the Elohimites, see Palmer 2004.

Chapter 1

1. Literary realism was a nineteenth-century movement concerned primarily with giving matter-of-fact descriptions of social and psychological reality. Naturalism, which adopted the basic approach of the realist tradition but added its own unique posits, presented a view of human nature

according to which the actions of characters are determined by genetic and social conditions over which they have little control. In this respect, the term "naturalism" conveys not only a style of writing but also a philosophical commitment to a deterministic view of human nature, whereas the broad aim of the realist approach was to depict social and psychological reality with the greatest possible specificity and attention to detail. *The Elementary Particles* drew immediate comparison with Zola and naturalism. See Badré 1998.

2. Descartes famously proposed that mind and body were composed of two intrinsically different substances, one material and the other immaterial. The first, res extensa, occupied the world of physical, "extended" space, while the other, res cogitans, belonged to an internal, immaterial world of thought that existed outside of the physical realm (though still interacted with it).

3. The Copenhagen interpretation of quantum physics holds that no clear dividing line exists between the observer and what is being observed. See Wolf 1989, 128–29.

4. According to the principle of nonseparability, two particles can, under certain conditions, exercise a nonlocal effect on each other. That is, the action of each particle will affect the other regardless of the distance between them.

5. See Berger 1997; Demerath 2007; Hadden 1987; Hervieu-Léger 1990; Lechner 1991; Martin 1991; Stark 1999; Stark and Iannaccone 1994; Wilson 1985; and Yamane 1997 for a broad-ranging, representative discussion of debates over secularization that have taken place since the 1980s.

6. Sociologist of religion Karel Dobbelaere (1987, 117) proposes a three-level analysis of secularization as a phenomenon occurring in the institutional, societal, and individual realms.

7. This passage may very well owe a debt to Arthur Schopenhauer, one of Houellebecq's avowed influences. In his essay "On Suicide" (2006), Schopenhauer argues that suicide, while not criminal or even explicitly prohibited in the Bible, nonetheless constitutes a *mistake.* To kill oneself thwarts what Schopenhauer contends is the highest moral aim of life—the suppression of the will to live. We are all driven forward to greater forms of becoming by the universal will that inhabits all of nature, and it is the will's frustration with its own limitations, its desire to escape the fetters of a finite form, that pushes the human being to suicide. The person who has overcome the will—who has overcome the instinct for becoming—will therefore have no need of suicide, for hopelessness has become impossible. Even so, Schopenhauer strongly condemns the criminalization of suicide, arguing that there is nothing to which we have a greater right than our life and person. Though not explicitly stated, such reasoning surely informs Jean-Pierre's decision—just as it does those European governments that have legalized euthanasia.

8. It is also worth mentioning that Houellebecq's portrayal of struggling, isolated priests was nothing new in twentieth-century French literature. Georges Bernanos, for example, is well known for his novel *The Diary of a Country Priest*, which depicts the wretched material and moral conditions in which a young priest in 1930s

northern France is forced to live: "It is hard to be alone, and harder still to share your solitude with indifferent or ungrateful people" (35). François Mauriac offers a similar image of the lonely priest in this passage from his 1927 novel, *Thérèse Desqueyroux*: "Based on some things Jean Azevedo had said, Thérèse began to pay more attention to this still-young priest who didn't communicate much with his parishioners. They thought he was arrogant: 'He's not the type we want around here.' During his rare visits to the de la Traves, Thérèse observed his whitening temples, his high forehead. No friends. How did he spend his evenings? Why had he chosen this life?" (2005, 81).

9. I address Houellebecq's shift from atheism to agnosticism in my final chapter.

Chapter 2

1. The novel follows the lives of three Daniels, the first an aging comedian living in twenty-first-century Europe and the others the twenty-fourth and twenty-fifth in a series of clones of the original. Chapters devoted to the original Daniel are titled Daniel1.1, Daniel1.2, and so on, while those concerned with the two clones are rendered Daniel24.1, Daniel25.1, and so forth, resembling the numbering of chapters and verses in the Bible. See Cuenebroeck 2011 for a discussion.

2. This and all subsequent quotations from Comte's work throughout this book are my own translations from the original French.

3. See, for instance, Benthall 2008; Smart 1996; and Taylor 2007.

4. Asad is specifically concerned with challenging the definition of religion that Clifford Geertz proposes in *The Interpretation of Cultures* (1973, 87–125).

5. I imagine this suggestion would elicit howls of desecration from the men and women involved in the "singularity" movement and other such cultish organizations in Silicon Valley. For an interesting analysis of current trends, see Sam Frank's article "Come with Us If You Want to Live: Among the Apocalyptic Libertarians of Silicon Valley," in the January 2015 issue of *Harper's Magazine.*

6. I nevertheless wonder if it is truly fair to use the term "Islamophobia" to condemn biases against Islam that arise in reaction to certain aspects of the religion. Certainly it makes sense to be fearful of the practices of more conservative forms of Islam, such as stoning adulterers, hanging homosexuals, or cutting off the hands of thieves. Similarly, I feel a certain alarm when I encounter fundamentalist Christians who want to outlaw abortion, reinstate mandatory school prayer, and teach creationism in schools. Do such feelings make me a bigot? It is possible that those with the greatest fear of fundamentalist Islam in the world today are women living in Taliban-occupied Pakistan and Iraq, or homosexuals in Iran; should we also condemn them as intolerant and bigoted?

Chapter 3

1. The phrase "the fresh ruins of France" is a quotation from Edmund Burke's *Reflections of the Revolution in France*: "The fresh ruins of France,

which shock our feelings wherever we can turn our eyes, are not the devastation of civil war; they are the sad but instructive monuments of rash and ignorant counsel in time of profound peace" (Burke 1984, 41).

2. All subsequent passages from Robespierre in this chapter are also my translation.

3. Of the four social reformers I cite, Robespierre is perhaps of greatest interest to scholars today, given his connection not simply with religious configurations of utopia (the Cult of the Supreme Being), but also with state terror and terrorism more generally. See Žižek 2007 for a discussion. Comte also remains of contemporary interest in France. See, for instance, Bourdeau et al. 2003; and Sartori 2004.

4. The centerpiece of Fourier's system was the *phalanstère*, or phalanx, a sort of "grand hotel" in which a set number of persons—1,620 was the ideal number—would be grouped according to specific personality traits. Fourier theorized the existence of 810 distinct kinds of personality; thus, in a community of 1,620 persons, each member would have at least one person of the same personality type. Fourier was intensely systematic in his prescriptions for the ideal community, and his distaste for "civilization," as he referred to industrial and liberal modernity, seems to have known no bounds.

5. Subsequent passages from Fourier 1953 and 1967 also are my translation.

6. All subsequent passages from Saint-Simon are also my translation.

7. Apropos of his own atheism, Houellebecq complains to Lévy of "the feeling, exhausting in the long run, that one is a vague organic hodgepodge whose controls are gradually failing" (2011, 164).

8. Schopenhauer expounds his moral philosophy in his long essay *On the Basis of Morality* (1995). For an analysis, especially regarding Schopenhauer's disagreement with Kant, see Cartwright 1999.

9. See, in particular, Coppée 1897; and Retté 1907.

Chapter 4

1. The hagiographic texts of Bardolle 2004 and Noguez 2003 might be said to offer two examples of such a reading.

2. One could also say much about the Elohim here, who the Elohimites in *Possibility* claim are responsible for the creation of life on earth. A crucial difference is that, while creatures such as Yog-Sothoth are real enough in Lovecraft's tales, it is never seriously considered in *Possibility* that the Elohim should actually exist, except by the clones who have imbibed their cult's propaganda.

3. This observation also helps to distinguish Houellebecq's fiction from science fiction. Houellebecq certainly engages themes that are beholden to science fiction (posthumanism, cloning, etc.), but he does so in service of religious and existential concerns. The goal of Houellebecq's treatment of science is not to explore the social, ethical, or religious questions that advances in science pose (a typical trope in science fiction writing), but rather to ask what the value we place in science as "progress" tells us about our religious and existential assumptions today.

Chapter 5

1. All translations from *Soumission* are my own from the original French. I have chosen to render the title as *Submission* in the main text.

2. For instance, Manuel Valls, the French prime minister, said after the attacks, "La France n'est pas Michel Houellebecq. [. . .] ça n'est pas l'intolérance, la haine, la peur" (France is not Michel Houellebecq. [. . .] it is not intolerance, hatred, and fear; Leyris 2015, n.p.). It is also worth noting that *Soumission* was unfairly conflated with Éric Zemmour's *Le suicide français* (2014), a very long essay on the "decline of France" that much more polemically, ideologically, and, of course, negatively engages the question of the "great replacement" that Islam allegedly represents. For a discussion of Pegida's reaction to *Soumission*, see Trierweiler 2015.

3. It may be that Houellebecq is conjuring up Bruno from *The Elementary Particles*, whose wife's name is Anne (so similar to Annelise). The marriage between Bruno and Anne is predictably unhappy, ending in divorce after Bruno commits an act of pedophilia.

4. See, for example, Helen Smith's *Men on Strike: Why Men Are Boycotting Marriage, Fatherhood, and the American Dream—and Why It Matters* (2014); Kay S. Hymowitz's *Manning Up: How the Rise of Women Has Turned Men into Boys* (2012); and Christina Hoff Summer's *The War Against Boys: How Misguided Policies Are Harming Our Young Men* (2013). It is worth noting that all three authors are women.

5. In the original French version, "fuck autonomy" is rendered in English.

6. For a discussion of Huysmans's aesthetic considerations in relation to his conversion, see Hanson 1997, 108–68, esp. 126–37.

7. This is a paraphrase of Barbey D'Aurevilly, who wrote apropos of *À rebours* in *Le roman contemporain* (the original essay appeared elsewhere in 1884): "Je serais bien capable de porter à l'auteur d'*À rebours* le même défi: 'Après *Les Fleurs du mal*,—dis-je à Baudelaire,—il ne vous reste plus, logiquement, que la bouche d'un pistolet ou les pieds de la croix.' Baudelaire choisit les pieds de la croix. Mais l'auteur d'*À rebours* les choisira-t-il?" (I could very well make a similar challenge to the author of *À rebours*: "After *Les Fleurs du mal*, I said to Baudelaire, the only logical choice you have left is between the mouth of a pistol and the feet of the cross." Baudelaire chose the feet of the cross. But will the author of *À rebours* choose them?) D'Aurevilly 1902, 281–82.

8. Houellebecq's treatment of academic upheaval in the French university scene is accompanied by some waggish critiques of professorial psychology. He writes, "Those who become university professors never even imagine that a political development could have the slightest effect on their career; they feel absolutely untouchable" (79). With growing calls from the American right to reform tenure and to roll back shared governance (a call that has already become reality in the state of Wisconsin, where I hold a faculty position), I wonder—and worry—how prescient Houellebecq's comments will be!

9. I am speaking, of course, of the western Roman Empire; the eastern empire, centered in Constantinople,

survived well into the fifteenth century, although it is more commonly referred to as Byzantium.

10. Works published by the Bibliothèque de la Pléiade are broadly considered to represent the authoritative scholarly editions of work by major French authors. For a scholar to be asked to edit a Pléiade book is thus understood as a recognition by the French intellectual community that he or she is the preeminent expert on a given subject.

11. It is telling that François's decision to convert appears linked to a desire to reaffirm his threatened virility. However, to reduce his motivation to the need for sex—and thus in some respects to portray Islam's attractiveness in the novel as predicated not on spirituality but rather on sexuality—is unwarranted. François visits numerous prostitutes in *Submission*, making it clear that in converting to Islam he is in search of something more than just carnal adventure. Moreover, there is nothing surprising or transgressive in the idea that religions should regulate sexual practices; since these are tied to and determine domestic and family life, religion, as a socially-structuring institution grounded in divine sanction, naturally seeks to exert control over them.

WORKS CITED

Armand, Félix. 1953. Introduction to *Textes choisis* by Charles Fourier, 7–43. Paris: Éditions Sociales.

Asad, Talal. 1993. *Genealogies of Religion: Discipline and Reasons of Power in Christianity and Islam.* Baltimore: Johns Hopkins University Press.

Badré, Frédéric. 1998. "Une nouvelle tendance en littérature." *Le Monde*, October 3.

Bardolle, Olivier. 2004. *La littérature à vif (le cas Houellebecq).* Paris: L'Ésprit des péninsules.

Beecher, Jonathan. 1990. *Charles Fourier: A Visionary and His World.* Berkeley: University of California Press.

Bellanger, Aurélien. 2010. *Houellebecq, écrivain romantique.* Paris: Éditions Léo Scheer.

Benthall, Jonathan. 2008. *Returning to Religion.* London: I. B. Tauris.

Berger, Peter. 1967. *The Sacred Canopy.* New York: Anchor.

———. 1997. "Epistemological Modesty: An Interview with Peter Berger." *Christian Century*, October 20.

Bernanos, Georges. 1937. *The Diary of a Country Priest.* Cambridge, Mass.: Da Capo.

Betty, Louis. 2012. "Michel Houellebecq, Meet Maximilien Robespierre: A Study in Social Religion." *L'Érudit Franco-Espagnol* 1 (1): 19–33. http://lef-e.org/yahoo_site_admin/assets/docs/Betty_June_2012.348133504.pdf.

———. 2013. "Classical Secularization Theory in Contemporary Literature: The Curious Case of Michel Houellebecq." *Literature and Theology* 27 (1): 98–115.

Bonnefous, Bastien. 2015. "François Hollande, le risque de la répétition." *Le Monde*, January 6. http://www.lemonde.fr/politique/article/2015/01/05/francois-hollande-le-risque-de-la-repetition_4549231_823448.html.

Bourdeau, Michel, et al., eds. 2003. *Auguste Comte aujourd'hui.* Paris: Éditions Kimé.

Burke, Edmund. 1984. "Reflections on the Revolution in France." In *Burke, Paine, Godwin, and the Revolution Controversy*, ed. Marilyn Butler, 33–48. Cambridge: Cambridge University Press.

Calvet, Jean. 1927. *Le renouveau catholique dans la littérature contemporaine.* Paris: F. Lanore.

Cartwright, David E. 1999. "Schopenhauer's Narrower Sense of Morality." In *The Cambridge Companion to Schopenhauer*, ed. Christopher Janaway, 252–92.

Cambridge: Cambridge University Press.
Chabert, George. 2002. "Michel Houellebecq: Lecteur d'Auguste Comte." *Revue Romane* 37 (2): 187–204.
Chaigne, Louis. 1940. *Anthologie de la renaissance catholique.* Paris: Éditions Alsatia.
Chassay, Jean-François. 2005. "Les Corpuscules de Krause: À propos des *Particules élémentaires* de Michel Houellebecq." *Australian Journal of French Studies* 42 (1): 36–49.
Chaves, Mark. 1994. "Secularization as Declining Religious Authority." *Social Forces* 72 (3): 749–74.
Clément, Murielle Lucie. 2006. "Le héros houellebecquien." *Studi Francesi* 50 (1): 91–99.
Compagnon, Antoine. 2005. *Les anti-modernes.* Paris: Gallimard.
Comte, Auguste. 1968. "Discours préliminaire sur l'ensemble du positivisme." In *Oeuvres d'Auguste Comte*, 7:1–399. Paris: Éditions Anthropos.
Coppée, François. 1897. *La bonne souffrance.* Paris: Librairie Alphonse Lemerre.
Cruickshank, Ruth. 2003. "L'Affaire Houellebecq: Ideological Crime and Fin de Millénaire Literary Scandal." *French Cultural Studies* 41 (1): 101–16.
Cuenebroeck, Fanny van. 2011. "Michel Houellebecq ou la possibilité d'une bible." In *Michel Houellebecq à la une*, ed. Murielle Lucie Clément and Sabine van Wesemael, 221–31. Amsterdam: Rodopi.
Dahan-Gaida, Laurence. 2003. "La fin de l'histoire (naturelle): *Les particules élémentaires* de Michel Houellebecq." *Tangence* 73:93–114.
D'Aurevilly, Barbey. 1902. *Le roman contemporain.* Paris: Alphonse Lemerre.
Demerath, N. J., III. 2007. "Secularization and Sacralization Deconstructed and Reconstructed." In *Sage Handbook of the Sociology of Religion*, ed. James A. Beckford and N. J. Demerath III, 57–80. Los Angeles: Sage.
Dobbelaere, Karel. 1987. "Some Trends in European Sociology of Religion: The Secularization Debate." *Sociological Analysis* 48 (2): 107–37.
Doré, Kim. 2002. "Doléances d'un surhomme ou la question de l'évolution dans *Les particules élémentaires* de Michel Houellebecq." *Tangence* 70:67–83.
Durkheim, Émile. 1994. *Durkheim on Religion: A Selection of Readings with Bibliographies.* Ed. W. S. F. Pickering. Atlanta: Scholars Press.
European Commission. 2005. *Special Eurobarometer 225: Social Values, Science, and Technology.* http://ec.europa.eu/public_opinion/archives/ebs/ebs_225_report_en.pdf.
Fourier, Charles. 1953. *Textes choisis.* Ed. Félix Armand. Paris: Éditions Sociales.
———. 1967. *La théorie des quatre mouvements.* Paris: J.-J. Pauvert.
———. 1996. *The Theory of the Four Movements.* Cambridge: Cambridge University Press.

Gantz, Katherine. 2005. "Strolling with Houellebecq: The Textual Terrain of Postmodern *flânerie.*" *Journal of Modern Literature* 28 (3): 149–61.

Geertz, Clifford. 1973. *The Interpretation of Cultures.* New York: Basic.

Gopnik, Adam. 2015. "The Next Thing: Michel Houellebecq's Francophobic Satire." *New Yorker*, January 26.

Gugelot, Frédéric. 1998. *La conversion des intellectuels au catholicisme en France, 1885–1935.* Paris: CRNS.

Hadden, Jeffrey K. 1987. "Toward Desacralizing Secularization Theory." *Social Forces* 65 (3): 587–611.

Hanson, Ellis. 1997. *Decadence and Catholicism.* Cambridge: Harvard University Press.

Hervieu-Léger, Danièle. 1990. "Religion and Modernity in the French Context: For a New Approach to Secularization." *Sociological Analysis* 51:15–25.

Hofmann, Pauline. 2015. "France, Allemagne, Italie: Michel Houellebecq fait un carton." *Europe1*, February 10. http://www.europe1.fr/livres/soumission-de-houellebecq-best-seller-dans-trois-pays-2369577.

Houellebecq, Michel. 1998. Interview by Catherine Argand. *Lire*, September 1. http://www.lexpress.fr/culture/livre/michel-houellebecq_802424.html.

———. 2000a. *The Elementary Particles.* New York: Vintage International.

———. 2000b. *Lanzarote.* London: Vintage.

———. 2001. Interview by Didier Sénécal. *Lire*, December 1. http://www.lexpress.fr/culture/livre/plateforme_805352.html.

———. 2002. *Platform.* New York: Vintage International.

———. 2005. *H. P. Lovecraft: Against the World, Against Life.* San Francisco: Believer Books.

———. 2007. *The Possibility of an Island.* New York: Vintage International.

———. 2009. *Interventions II.* Paris: Flammarion.

———. 2010. "Michel Houellebecq: The Art of Fiction no. 206." Interview by Susannah Hunnewell. *Paris Review* 194. http://www.theparisreview.org/interviews/6040/the-art-of-fiction-no-206-michel-houellebecq.

———. 2011. *Whatever.* London: Serpent's Tail.

———. 2012. *The Map and the Territory.* New York: Knopf.

———. 2015a. *Soumission.* Paris: Gallimard.

———. 2015b. "Scare Tactics: Michel Houellebecq on His New Book." Interview by Sylvain Bourmeau. *Paris Review*, January 6. http://www.theparisreview.org/blog/2015/01/02/scare-tactics-michel-houellebecq-on-his-new-book/.

Houellebecq, Michel, and Bernard-Henri Lévy. 2011. *Public Enemies.* New York: Random House.

Hungerford, Amy. 2010. *Postmodern Belief: American Literature and*

Religion Since 1960. Princeton: Princeton University Press.
Israel, Jonathan. 2002. *Radical Enlightenment*. New York: Oxford University Press.
Jeffery, Ben. 2011. *Anti-Matter: Michel Houellebecq and Depressive Realism*. Winchester, England: Zero.
Johnson, Michael A., and Lawrence R. Schehr, eds. 2009. "Turns to the Right?" Special issue, *Yale French Studies* 116–17.
Jones, Gareth Stedman, and Ian Patterson. 1996. Introduction to *The Theory of the Four Movements* by Charles Fourier, vii–xxvi. Cambridge: Cambridge University Press.
Joshi, S. T. 2008. Introduction to *H. P. Lovecraft: The Complete Fiction*, ix–xiv. New York: Barnes and Noble.
Jourde, Pierre. 2002. *La littérature sans estomac*. Paris: L'Esprit des Péninsules.
Kakutani, Michiko. 2000. "Unsparing Case Studies of Humanity's Vileness." *New York Times*, November 10. http://www.nytimes.com/2000/11/10/books/books-of-the-times-unsparing-case-studies-of-humanity-s-vileness.html.
Kant, Immanuel. 1990. *Critique of Pure Reason*. Amherst, N.Y.: Prometheus.
Lechner, Frank J. 1991. "The Case Against Secularization: A Rebuttal." *Social Forces* 69 (4): 1103–19.
Lévy, Bernard-Henri. 2009. *Left in Dark Times*. Trans. Benjamin Moser. New York: Random House.
Leyris, Raphaëlle. 2015. "Le frappant téléscopage entre la sortie du livre de Houellebecq et l'attentat contre Charlie Hebdo." *Le Monde*, January 9. http://www.lemonde.fr/livres/article/2015/01/09/le-frappant-telescopage-entre-lasortie-du-livre-de-houellebecq-et-1-attentat-contre-charliehebdo_4552323_3260.html.
Lilla, Mark. 2015. "Slouching Toward Mecca." *New York Review of Books*, April 2. http://www.nybooks.com/articles/archives/2015/apr/02/slouching-toward-mecca.
Lindenberg, Daniel. 2002. *Le rappel à l'ordre*. Paris: Seuil.
Lipovetsky, Gilles. 2004. *Les temps hypermodernes*. Paris: Grasset.
Lloyd, Vincent. 2009. "Michel Houellebecq and the Theological Virtues." *Literature and Theology* 23 (1): 84–98.
Lovecraft, H. P. 2008. *The Complete Fiction*. New York: Barnes and Noble.
———. 2009. *At the Mountains of Madness: And Other Weird Tales*. New York: Barnes and Noble.
Manuel, Frank E., and Fritzie P. Manuel. 1979. *Utopian Thought in the Western World*. Cambridge, Mass.: Belknap.
Maris, Bernard. 2014. *Houellebecq économiste*. Paris: Flammarion.
Martin, David. 1991. "The Secularization Issue: Prospect and Retrospect." *British Journal of Sociology* 42 (3): 465–74.
Maslin, Janet. 2003. "Tourism, Sex, and a Generous Dose of Contempt." *New York Times*, July 21. http://

www.nytimes.com/2003/07/21/books/books-of-the-times-tourism-sex-and-a-generous-dose-of-contempt.html.

Maugham, W. Somerset. 1944. *The Razor's Edge.* New York: Doubleday, Doran.

Mauriac, François. 2005. *Thérèse Desqueyroux.* Lanham: Rowman and Littlefield.

McCann, John. 2011. *Michel Houellebecq: Author of Our Times.* Oxford: Peter Lang.

Meyronnis, François. 2007. *De l'extermination considérée comme un des beaux arts.* Paris: Gallimard.

Moore, Gerald. 2011. "Gay Science and (No) Laughing Matter: The Eternal Returns of Michel Houellebecq." *French Studies* 65 (1): 45–60.

Morrey, Douglas. 2013. *Michel Houellebecq: Humanity and Its Aftermath.* Liverpool: Liverpool University Press.

Morrison, Donald. 2010. *The Death of French Culture.* Cambridge, England: Polity.

Muray, Philippe. 1999. "Et, en tout, apercevoir la fin." *L'Atelier du Roman*, June 18.

Noguez, Dominique. 2003. *Houellebecq, en fait.* Paris: Fayard.

Palmer, Susan J. 2004. *Aliens Adored: Rael's UFO Religion.* New Brunswick: Rutgers University Press.

Pascal, Blaise. 1995. *Pensées and Other Writings.* New York: Oxford World's Classics.

Pew Forum. 2011. *The Future of the Global Muslim Population: Region: Europe.* January 27. http://www.pewforum.org/2011/01/27/future-of-the-global-muslim-population-regional-europe/.

Pfaff, Steven. 2008. "The Religious Divide: Why Religion Seems to Be Thriving in the United States and Waning in Europe." In *Growing Apart? America and Europe in the Twenty-First Century*, ed. Jeffrey Kopstein, 24–52. New York: Cambridge University Press.

Rabosseau, Sandrine. 2007. "Houellebecq ou le renouveau du roman experimental." In *Michel Houellebecq sous la loupe*, ed. Murielle Lucie Clément and Sabine van Wesemael, 43–51. Amsterdam: Rodopi.

Retté, Adolphe. *Du diable à Dieu: Histoire d'une conversion.* Paris: L. Vanier and A. Messein, 1907.

Ricard, François. 1999. "Le Roman contre le monde: Houellebecq, Muray, Duteurtre." *Liberté* 41 (3): 48–56.

Riding, Alan. 1999. "Roman a Gripe Stirs Flames Among French." *New York Times*, March 2. http://www.nytimes.com/1999/03/02/books/arts-abroad-roman-a-gripe-stirs-flames-among-french.html.

Robespierre, Maximilien. 1989. *Écrits.* Ed. Claude Mazauric. Paris: Messidor/Éditions Sociales.

Roth, Zoë. 2012. "The Death of Desire: Bataille, Transgression, and the Erotic Extreme in Michel Houellebecq's *Plateforme.*" In *Autour de l'extrême littéraire*, ed. Alastair Hemmens and Russell Williams, 112–23. Newcastle upon Tyne: Cambridge Scholars.

Sageret, Jules. 1906. *Les grands convertis*. Paris: Société du Mercure de France.
Saint-Simon, Claude Henri de. 1997. "Nouveau christianisme." In *Saint-Simon: Oeuvres complètes*, vol. 3. Geneva: Slatkine Reprints.
Sartori, Eric. 2004. "Michel Houellebecq, romancier positiviste." In *Michel Houellebecq*, ed. Sabine van Wesemael, 143–51. Amsterdam: Rodopi.
Sartre, Jean-Paul. 2007. *Existentialism Is a Humanism*. New Haven: Yale University Press.
Schopenhauer, Arthur. 1995. *On the Basis of Morality*. Providence, R.I.: Berghahn.
———. 2006. *Suffering, Suicide, and Immortality: Eight Essays from the Parerga*. Mineola, N.Y.: Dover.
Smart, Ninian. 1996. *Dimensions of the Sacred: An Anatomy of the World's Beliefs*. Berkeley: University of California Press.
Stark, Rodney. 1999. "Secularization, R.I.P." *Sociology of Religion* 60 (3): 249–73.
———. 2004. *Exploring the Religious Life*. Baltimore: Johns Hopkins University Press.
Stark, Rodney, and Laurence Iannaccone. 1994. "A Supply-Side Reinterpretation of the 'Secularization' of Europe." *Journal for the Scientific Study of Religion* 30:230–52.
Sweeney, Carole. 2013. *Michel Houellebecq and the Literature of Despair*. London: Bloomsbury.
Taylor, Bron. 2007. "Exploring Religion, Nature, and Culture—Introducing the *Journal for the Study of Religion, Nature, and Culture*." *Journal for the Study of Religion, Nature, and Culture* 1 (1): 5–24.
Todorov, Tzvetan. 2007. *La littérature en péril*. Paris: Flammarion.
Trierweiler, Denis. 2015. "Pegida, Charlie et Houellebecq." *Paris Match*, January 16. http://www.parismatch.com/Actu/International/Pegida-Charlie-et-Houellebecq-692122.
Updike, John. 2006. "90% Hateful." *New Yorker*, May 26. http://www.newyorker.com/archive/2006/05/22/060522crbo_books?printable=true.
van Wesemael, Sabine. 2005. *Michel Houellebecq, le plaisir du texte*. Paris: L'Harmattan.
Varsava, Jerry. 2005. "Utopian Yearnings, Dystopian Thoughts: Houellebecq's *The Elementary Particles* and the Problem of Scientific Communitarianism." *College Literature* 32 (5): 145–67.
Vertaldi, Aurélia. 2015. "Hollande lira *Soumission* de Houellebecq car 'il fait débat.'" *Le Figaro*, January 5. http://www.lefigaro.fr/livres/2015/01/05/03005-20150105ARTFIG00131-hollande-lira-soumission-de-houellebecq-car-il-fait-debat.php.
Viard, Bruno. 2008. *Houellebecq au laser: La faute à Mai 68*. Nice: Ovadia.
———. 2013a. *Littérature et déchirure: De Montaigne à Houellebecq*. Paris: Classiques Garnier.
———. 2013b. *Les tiroirs de Michel Houellebecq*. Paris: Presses Universitaires de France.

Voas, David. 2009. "The Rise and Fall of Fuzzy Fidelity in Europe." *European Sociological Review* 25 (2): 155–69.

Wilson, Bryan. 1985. "Secularization: The Inherited Model." In *The Sacred in a Secular Age: Toward Revision in the Scientific Study of Religion*, ed. Phillip E. Hammond, 9–20. Berkeley: University of California Press.

Wolf, Fred Alan. 1989. *Taking the Quantum Leap: The New Physics for Nonscientists.* New York: Perennial Library.

Yamane, David. 1997. "Secularization on Trial: In Defense of a Neosecularization Paradigm." *Journal for the Scientific Study of Religion* 36 (1): 109–22.

Zemmour, Éric. 2014. *Le suicide français.* Paris: Albin Michel.

Žižek, Slavoj. 2007. Introduction to *Robespierre: Virtue and Terror*, vii–xxxix. London: Verso.

INDEX

Against the World, Against Life, 117
description of Lovecraftian cosmos, 105. *See also* Lovecraft, Howard Phillips
introduction to, 114
Althusser, 75, 77
American reception of Houellebecq, 13
atheism
atheistic humanism, 11, 76, 130, 135, 139
Daniel's atheism in *The Possibility of An Island*, 20
Houellebecq on, 45, 129, 146 n. 7
Rediger on, 135–36

Bataille, 3
Baudelaire, 3, 142, 147 n. 7
Beauvoir, Simone de, 84
Bernanos, Georges, 144–45 n. 8
Bourdieu, 75
Bourget, Paul, 101
Brunnetière, Ferdinand, 101
Burke, Edmund, 145–46 n. 1

Camus, 13, 77
Carnap, Rudolf, 22
Catholicism
Catholic renaissance, 101–3
Comte on, 90
conversion to Catholicism: in *Submission*, 129–30, 132; in *The Map and the Territory*, 102
decline of Catholicism, 31, 139; in France, 42–45
depiction of Catholic priests, 144–45 n. 8; in *The Map and the Territory*, 44; in *Whatever*, 31, 43–45
and Islam, 131
return to Catholicism, 16
Charlie Hebdo, 71, 122–23
Christianity
Comte on, 50, 94–95
decline of Christianity in Europe, 33–34, 46, 60, 135, 139
early, parallel with Elohimism, 64.
and Elohimism, 31, 35, 72
and Islam, 52, 73, 123
medieval Christianity, 88, 139–40
Saint-Simon on, 77, 86–89
similarities with Islam, 130
Claudel, Paul, 101
Comte, 33, 47, 95–97, 140
on the decline of Christianity, 50, 94–95
on eternal life, 49–50, 91
Houellebecq's critique of Comte's ideas about eternal life, 50–51, 91–92
law of the three stages, 89
perception of Catholicism, 90
on religion, 49
religion of humanity, 3, 16, 49–50, 78, 90
on rights, 92–93. *See also* Fourier
Viard on, 3
view of monotheism, 90
on women, 93–94
Coppée, François, 101–2

Dantec, Maurice, 3
D'Aurevilly, Barbey, 147 n. 7
Descartes, 22, 144 n. 2
Diderot, 78
Durkheim, 15
definition of religion, 47, 51
sacred and the profane, the, 59, 63–64
Duteurtre, Benoît, 3

Elementary Particles, The
Americanization, 8–10
Annabelle, 21, 37–38, 40, 104, 116
Annick, 21, 39–40
Asad's theories of religion, as mise-en-scène of, 60
Bruno: on life after death, 39; sexual obsession, 37
Christiane, 36–37, 40, 82
Cruickshank on, 2
Desplechin, 12, 33
Djerzinski: on religion, 33; on women, 83, 93
escape from materialism, 29-30. *See also* materialism
Kakutani on, 13
Lieu du Changement, 36
meaning of use of quantum physics, 29. *See also* quantum physics
Meditations on Interweaving, 29, 87
Muray on, 105
and naturalism, 144 n. 1. *See also* Naturalism
Elohimism, 15–16, 97
disciplinary aspect of, 68–70
doctrine of, 61–63, 146 n. 2
and euthanasia, 58
immortality, 48, 61, 64–65
and Islam, 71–73
and materialism, 48–49, 52
parallel with early Christianity, 64
and positivism, 50
prophet of, 61, 64
and "religare," 60–63
rise of, 31, 35, 48, 57, 79
and the sacred and the profane, 63–64. *See also* Durkheim
suicide ritual, 64. *See also* suicide
and the supernatural, 64–66
Engels, 77
Enlightenment, 133, 139–41
critique of, 135, 141
and the decline of Christianity, 94. *See also* Christianity
and Islam, 139. *See also* Islam
radical enlightenment, 78
shortcomings of, 17, 123, 140
euthanasia
of the elderly, 48, 57
and Elohimism, 58
legality of euthanasia, 144 n. 1
opposition to, 41–42. *See also* Schopenhauer

feminism, 6, 127
antifeminism, 3
and de Beauvoir, 84
and Fourier, 82
Sweeney on, 143 n. 1
Flaubert, 22. *See also* Realism
Foucault, 13, 75–76
Fourier, 14, 16, 77–78, 96–97, 146 n. 4
affinities with Saint-Simon, 89
on children and child-rearing, 84–85
on human rights, 85
and Marx, 95
on numerical organization of utopia, 85–86
on sexuality, 80–82
on women, 82–84
Frankfurt School, 136

Glucksmann, André, 76

Hegel, G. W. F., 22

Houellebecq (character), 17–18
conversion to Catholicism in *The Map and the Territory*, 102. *See also* Catholicism
humanism
atheistic humanism, 11, 76, 130, 135, 139
secular humanism, 73
Huysmans, Joris-Karl, 101, 134, 136
conversion to Catholicism, 129, 132. *See also* Catholicism

Interventions II
"Approches du désarroi," 34
erotic hierarchy, 10, 80
"J'ai un rêve," 91
"L'humanité, second stade," 84
"Préliminaires au positivism," 49
Proguidis, Lakis, 24, 30
Solanas, Valerie, 84, 93–94
Islam, 13, 52, 91
as alternative to atheistic humanism, 124. *See also* humanism
collapse of in *The Possibility of An Island*, 31, 35, 57, 73
conversion to, 17, 128, 132, 134–36
Elohimism as alternative to, 16, 72–73. *See also* Elohimism
"great replacement," 135
Islamicization, 71, 100, 122
Islamic State, 141
Islamophobia, 17, 71, 123, 145 n. 6
Lévi-Strauss on, 71
medieval Islam, 140
and Positivism, 139
Quran, 71
similarity with Christianity, 130
Spinoza on, 71
"stupidest religion" comment, 71, 123
and women, 125, 127–28

Kant, 26, 92, 119

La Mettrie, Julien Offray de, 78
Lanzarote, 143 n. 6
Le Pen, Marine, 122, 131
Lévy, Bernard-Henri, 76, 143 n. 7
Littell, Jonathan, 3
Lovecraft, Howard Phillips, 143 n. 7, 146 n. 6
origins of materialist horror, 113–17

Maistre, Joseph de, 142
Maoism, 75–76
Map and the Territory, The
capitalism of the countryside, 16, 100
and Catholic renaissance, 102. *See also* Catholicism
Châtelus-le-Marcheix, 99
contents of fictional Houellebecq's library, 95
conversion to Catholicism, 102. *See also* Catholicism
depiction of Catholic priests, 44. *See also* Catholicism
euthanasia of Jean-Pierre Martin, 41–42. *See also* euthanasia
and evolution of Houellebecq's work, 13, 16, 103
immigration, 13, 100
Martin's final art project, 12, 104
Marxism, 11, 75–76, 89
Marx, 22, 76–78, 95
Marx and Fourier, 96
materialism
"age of materialism," 11, 29, 60, 88
Bellanger on, 4
comparison with Islam, 71. *See also* Islam
and Elohimism, 48, 52, 56. *See also* Elohimism
Jeffery on, 5
materialist horror: and Lovecraft, 113–17; and moral secularization, 43, 45; and Pascal, 117–20; and sexual liberalism,

10; as experimental approach to literature, 105; Houellebecq's use of term, 143 n. 7; instances of, 105–9 (See also *Whatever*)
metaphysics of materialism, 87
and Newtonian mechanics, 29–30, 87
postmaterialism in *The Elementary Particles*, 29–30. See also *The Elementary Particles*
principal experimental condition of Houellebecq's work, 22, 46
relation to: capitalism, 4, 8–12; suicide, 35–42 (*See also* suicide)
and Robespierre, 78–79
Maugham, Somerset, 103
Mauriac, François, 101
Millet, Richard, 3

National Front, 71, 122
Naturalism
and *The Elementary Particles*, 144 n. 1
and Huysmans, 129
literary, 143–44 n. 1
and Zola, 22
Neurath, Otto, 22
Nietzsche, 3, 22
Djerzinski on, 92
Houellebecq on, 93, 119
Nouveaux philosophes, 76

Pascal, 15, 17, 112–13
origins of materialist horror, 117–20. *See also* materialism
Péguy, Charles, 101
Platform
Colombani on, 109
Eldorador Aphrodite, 82, 97
erotic philanthropy, 82. *See also* Fourier
on Islam, 71–72, 91
Maslin on, 13
Robert, 14
sex tourism, 6, 82
Valérie, 72, 97
on Western sexuality, 110–12
political correctness, 3, 13
Positivism, 4, 14, 86, 89
in Brazil, 96
Houellebecq's utopia as mise-en-scène of Positivism, 16
and Islam, 139
and materialism, 49. *See also* Comte
positivist catechism, 90. *See also* Comte
Possibility of An Island, The
Biblical structure, 3, 48, 145 n. 1
Esther, 14, 54–56, 58, 60
euthanasia, 48, 57, 64. *See also* euthanasia
"Future Ones," 62, 69, 97
"human savages," 57–58, 68, 70, 116
Isabelle, 53–54, 56, 61
"life story," 57, 62, 69, 97, 116, 119
as mise-en-scène of Asad's theories of religion, 60, 68–71,
Miskiewicz, 48, 64–65
Nazism, 53–54
prophet, 61, 64
Supreme Sister, 62, 68–69, 92
Updike on, 13
posthumanism, 13
comparison with prehumanism, 98
Morrey on, 2
posthuman clone society of *The Possibility of An Island*, 16
Public Enemies
Colombani's review of *Platform*, 109
Houellebecq's childhood encounter with Pascal, 118. *See also* Pascal
Houellebecq's denial of the materialist label, 23

Public Enemies (continued)
Houellebecq's relationship with Catholicism as a young man, 45

quantum physics, 23–26, 87
application to human biology, 15
Copenhagen Interpretation, 24, 26, 144 n. 3
Hilbert Space, 28–29
Uncertainty Principle, 26, 144 n. 3

Realism
and Flaubert, 22
and Lovecraft, 117
depressive realism, 5
issue of realism in Houellebecq's novels, 6, 110, 112
literary, 143 n. 1
Retté, Adolphe, 101–2
Robespierre, 3, 14–16, 126
and atheism, 79. *See also* atheism
contrast with Houellebecq, 79
Cult of the Supreme Being, 78–79, 90, 146 n. 3
Romanticism, 139–40
Rousseau, 78
Rushdie, Salman, 123
Russell, Bertrand, 22

sacredness, 7, 104
postmodern sacred, 7
sacred and the profane, the 59, 63–64. *See also* Durkheim
sacred canopy, 15
Saint-Simon, Claude-Henri de, 16, 77–78, 95–97
critique of Christianity, 86–87
individualism and decline of Christianity, 88–89. *See also* Christianity
on metaphysics, 87
nouveau christianisme, 77, 86, 89

Schopenhauer
moral philosophy, 93, 146 n. 8
on suicide, 144 n. 7. *See also* suicide
and the Supreme Sister, 69
on writing and style, 8
science fiction, 146 n. 3
secularization theory, 32–33, 42–43, 140
Berger on, 32
Houellebecq's novels as mise-en-scène of, 4, 15, 20
Spinoza 71, 78
Stalin, 76
Submission
Annelise, 126–27
Aurélie, 125
Bruno, 126–27
conversion: and Huysmans, 129–30, 132; and sexuality, 148 n. 11; meaning of François' conversion to Islam, 140–41; *Submission* as conversion narrative, 129; to Catholicism, 129–30 (*See also* Catholicism); to Islam, 132, 135–37 (*See also* Islam)
Gopnik on, 123, 141
Hollande, remarks by, 123
Lilla on, 124
Muslim Brotherhood, 127–29, 131–32, 141; and education, 132; and liberalism, 129; and women, 127-28
Myriam, 125–26
Pegida, 123, 147 n. 2
polygamy, 136–38
Rediger, 134–37, 139, 141; conversion to Islam, 13 (*See also* Islam); on intelligent design, 136; on polygamy, 137; on the suicide of Europe, 135 (*See also* suicide)
Rocamadour, 67, 132, 135, 139
Ten Questions About Islam, 136, 139
Valls on, 147 n. 2

suicide
of Annabelle, 21, 38, 40, 45
of Annick, 21, 38–40
of Christiane, 37, 39
and clones, 42
of Daniel, 55
of Djerzinski, 39
and Elohimism, 64
of Europe, 135
François, 130
link with materialism, 42. *See also* materialism
of Martin, Jean-Pierre, 41–42
Schopenhauer on, 144 n. 7. *See also* Schopenhauer

utopia
failure of, 92, 95–97
materialist utopia, 100
posthuman utopia, 12, 27
repudiation of, 13
sexual utopia, 81–82, 97
socialist utopians, 77
utopian socialism, 14, 16
utopian socialists, 96
van Wesemael, Sabine, on, 28

Vienna Circle, 22
Voltaire, 136

Whatever
animal fictions, 106, 108
Bardot, Brigitte, 106, 108–10, 112
Buvet, 31, 43–44. *See also* Catholicism
Catholic priests, 43–45. *See also* Catholicism
"Dialogues Between a Dachshund and a Poodle," 83
instances of materialist horror, 105–9. *See also* materialism
Lechardoy, 106, 108, 110
sexual pauperization, 9, 106, 110
Tisserand, 81, 106–8, 110, 112
Viard on, 2, 80
Wittgenstein, 22

Zemmour, Éric, 147 n. 2
Zola, 3, 5–6, 22
and Naturalism, 22. *See also* Naturalism

Typeset by
Regina Starace

Printed and bound by
Sheridan Books

Composed in
Charter ITC

Printed on
50# Natures Natural

Bound in
Arrestox

CPSIA information can be obtained
at www.ICGtesting.com
Printed in the USA
BVHW031359310820
587624BV00006B/139